T0326289

# HAKUIN ON KENSHO

# Hakuin
# on Kensho

## THE FOUR WAYS
## OF KNOWING

*Edited with commentary by*

## Albert Low

## SHAMBHALA
### BOULDER
2006

Shambhala Publications
2129 13th Street
Boulder, Colorado 80302
www.shambhala.com

Printed in the United States of America
Designed by Gopa & Ted2, Inc.

Shambhala Publications makes every effort to print on acid-free,
recycled paper.

Shambhala Publications is distributed worldwide by Penguin Random
House, Inc., and its subsidiaries.

Library of Congress Cataloging-in-Publication Data
Low, Albert.
Hakuin on kensho: the four ways of knowing/edited with
commentary by Albert Low.—1st ed.
p. cm.
Includes bibliographical references and index.
ISBN: 978-1-59030-377-1 (alk. paper)
1. Hakuin, 1686–1769. I. Title.
BQ9399.E597L69 2006
294.3'420427—dc22
2006013420

Dedicated to my first Zen Teacher,

Yasutani Roshi

# CONTENTS

# HAKUIN ON KENSHO

# Introduction

## Hakuin and the
## Importance of Awakening

At the beginning of his book *Wild Ivy*, the eighteenth-century Rinzai Zen master Hakuin says, "Anyone who would call himself a member of the Zen family must first of all achieve *kensho*—realization of the Buddha's way."[1] Throughout his life Hakuin would sound this clarion call, exhorting all who would listen to him to strive to their utmost to come to *kensho*, or awakening. He quoted Bodhidharma, who said:

> If someone without kensho makes a constant effort to keep his thoughts free and unattached, not only is he a great fool, he also commits a serious transgression against the dharma. He winds up in the passive indifference of empty emptiness, no more capable of distinguishing good from bad than a drunken man. If you want to put the dharma of non-activity into practice, you must put an end to all your thought attachments by breaking through into kensho. Unless you have kensho, you can never expect to attain a state of non-doing.[2]

Other Rinzai Zen masters stressed the importance of kensho as the jewel of Zen practice. Awakening was at the very heart of Buddha's teaching, and it distinguished his teaching from other teachings of his time. Even the illustrious Soto Zen teacher Keizan said, "Though there is nothing to give or receive, *satori* should be as conclusive as knowing your face by touching the nose."³

What sets Hakuin apart from other teachers is the vigor with which he pointed to the importance of kensho and the diligence with which he followed his own teaching. He laughed at teachers who scorned kensho as unnecessary or even impossible, saying, "[This kind of teacher] reminds you of someone who doesn't have the strength to raise his food up to his mouth to eat, yet who insists he isn't eating because the food is bad."⁴

A passionate defender of the Buddha's way, Hakuin could be vitriolic when talking of monks who were undisciplined and unappreciative of the dharma: "I have always loathed monks of their type. They are tiger fodder, no doubt about it. I hope one tears them into tiny shreds. The pernicious thieves—even if you killed off seven or eight of them every day, you would still remain totally blameless. Why are we so infested with them? Because the ancestral gardens have been neglected. They have run to seed. The verdant Dharma foliage has withered and only a wasteland remains."⁵

Hakuin's distain for the misleading guidance of Zen teachers who had not themselves attained kensho is reminiscent of Jesus's railing against the scribes and Pharisees in Matthew: "But woe to you, scribes and Pharisees, hypocrites! for you shut up the kingdom of heaven against men: for you enter not in *yourselves*, neither suffer you them that are entering to go in. . . . Woe unto you, scribes and Pharisees, hypocrites! for

you compass sea and land to make one proselyte, and when
he is become so, you make him twofold more a son of hell than
yourselves."[6]
Hakuin clearly recognized that "the practice of Zen is a for-
midable undertaking,"[7] and that because it is so difficult, many
fall short of the ultimate goal. Yet many who fall short become
teachers—and as a result, teach a dead form of *zazen,* or sitting meditation. Hakuin constantly argued against these teachers, and above all, against those who rejected koan practice.
He warned against "Zen people of today who are content to
sit quietly submerged at the bottom of their 'ponds of tranquil water,'" and who mislead their students by saying, "'Don't
dig into koans. Koans are quagmires. They will suck your self-
nature under. Have nothing to do with written words either.
Those are complicated tangle of vines that will grab hold of
your vital spirit and choke the life from it.'"[8]

## On Koan Study

Koan study starts with the breakthrough koans of "*Mu!*" or
"What was your face before your parents were born?" or, later,
Hakuin's own, "What is the sound of one hand clapping?"[9]
Koans are penetrating, traditional inquiries drawn from Buddhist teachings, as well as the sayings of the Zen patriarchs
and masters, that are paradoxical in nature and that point to
the nature of ultimate reality. They are called "breakthrough"
koans because, if we work with them, they can help us break
through the screen of habitual ideas and concepts into the clarity of the One Mind. After one has passed through the breakthrough koan, one works with several traditional collections of
koans to deepen and clarify one's realization. This method of

practice was first introduced into Zen Buddhism during the golden age of Zen, which lasted from about the sixth century until the tenth century. By the time of Hakuin, koan practice was in decline, and one of his great contributions was to revive koan study and make it once more a living part of the Zen way. For this reason, many Rinzai masters of today trace their dharma ancestry back to Hakuin.

Hakuin not only tirelessly advocated delving into the koans, he also insisted on the need to read and study the works of Buddhism, including the ancient Zen masters. His biographer, Torei, said, "The words and sayings of the Zen masters never left his side. He used them to illuminate the old teachings by means of the mind, to illuminate the mind by means of the old teachings."[10] Hakuin looked upon the practice of writing as "the exercise of verbal *prajna*"[11] (the aroused, unobstructed mind), which, no doubt, is why he did so much of it.

## HAKUIN'S PRACTICE

Hakuin was born in 1686 and by the age of fifteen was already ordained in the Zen tradition. He practiced what he taught and knew well the bitter struggles of Zen. At one time he became so disillusioned with Zen practice that he gave it up in favor of reading and studying contemporary Chinese and Japanese literature. Even so, he returned to the practice and continued his training until the age of thirty-five, when he began to teach, not only monks, but laypeople as well.

Like many people who go on and won't give up the practice of Zen, Hakuin was driven by great anxiety and anguish. This anguish afflicted him early in his life. He tells of one occasion when he was scared out of his wits by the hot water of the bath. He cried out to his mother in terror:

Mother, you don't understand. I can't even go into the bath without having my knees knock and my blood run cold. Just think what it will be like when I have to face the burning fires of hell all by myself. What am I going to do? Isn't there any way to escape? Do I have to sit back and wait calmly until death comes? If you know something, please tell me about it. I want to know everything! Have pity on me. Save me. This intolerable agony continues day and night— I can't bear it any longer.[12]

When he later became disillusioned with Zen, his acute anxiety was the cause. He had heard that the great Zen master Ganto had met a violent death at the hand of bandits, and, he wrote, "Wanting to learn more about the life of this priest, I got hold of a copy of *Praise of the True School,* and Kin and I read through it on our own. I learned that Yen-t'ou had met a violent death at the hands of bandits." This was a very disheartening discovery for Hakuin; Ganto was one in a million, "truly one of the dragons of his age." He wondered, if Ganto could be mugged and killed by bandits, "How could an ordinary, garden-variety monk like me hope to avoid falling into the three evil paths after I died? A Buddhist monk, I concluded, had to be the most useless creature on the face of the earth."[13] Hakuin rued the day that he had become a monk. He writes, "Look at me! A sorry, wretched-looking outcast. I can't possibly return to lay life—I'd be too ashamed. And it would be just as humiliating to sneak off somewhere and fling myself to a watery grave. One thing is sure, I am at the end of my religious quest. What a total, miserable failure I've become."[14]

For years he dwelt in meditation on the puzzle of Ganto's

death. Then, one day, he came to deep awakening and cried out, "I am Ganto!"

A famous story demonstrates that Hakuin's awakening indeed cured him of his terrible anxiety. A samurai visited him and asked, "Do heaven and hell really exist?"

"Who are you?" asked Hakuin.

"I am a samurai," the man replied.

"You, a warrior!" shouted Hakuin. "What kind of lord would employ you? You have a crafty look about you."

The samurai became so angry that he began to draw his sword.

Hakuin jeered, "So, you own a sword! It is probably much too blunt to hurt me."

The samurai drew out his sword. Hakuin said, "Here, open the gates of hell!"

Hearing this and recognizing the master's discipline, the samurai put his sword away and bowed.

"Here open the gates of paradise," said Hakuin.

Let us not forget that years of hard labor were necessary before Hakuin could be so free from his terror. His fear and anxiety drove him deep into his own nature to find the peace that he could not find outside.

## HAKUIN'S AWAKENINGS

When Hakuin was twenty-two, while he was attending talks on the sayings and writings of a Zen master, he came to his first awakening. This must have been what in Zen is called a "tongue-tip taste of Zen." Later, while he was reading, he had a much deeper awakening. Instead of causing him to abandon his practice, it prompted him to practice more intensely. He said that he "concentrated night and day on the *Mu* koan without a moment's rest."[15] Yet, he could not get any deeper realization. He went on practicing strenuously for another two years. He writes:

> Night and day I did not sleep; I forgot both to eat and rest. Suddenly a great doubt manifested itself before me. It was as though I were frozen solid in the midst of an ice sheet extending tens of thousands of miles. A purity filled my breast and I could neither go forward nor retreat. To all intents and purposes, I was out of my mind and the *Mu* alone remained. Although I sat in the lecture hall and listened to the master's lecture, it was as though I were hearing a discussion from a distance outside the hall. At times it felt as though I were floating through the air.[16]

Hakuin remained in this condition for several days. Then, he writes, "I chanced to hear the sound of the temple bell and I was suddenly transformed. It was as if a sheet of ice had been smashed or a jade tower had fallen with a crash."[17] All his former doubts "vanished as though ice had melted away." In a loud voice he called out, "Wonderful, wonderful. There is no cycle of birth and death through which one must pass. There is no enlightenment one must seek. The seventeen hundred koans handed down from the past have not the slightest value whatsoever."[18]

He then said something that will strike many people as strange if not downright outrageous. He said, "My pride soared up like a majestic mountain, my arrogance surged forward like the tide. Smugly I thought to myself: 'In the past two or three hundred years no one could have accomplished such a marvelous breakthrough as this.'" Shouldering his "glorious enlightenment," Hakuin set out at once for Shimano to call on Master Shinano.[19]

Most of us think that once someone is awakened, all illusions and faults—including all arrogance, pride, and conceit—are mysteriously wiped away. As we shall see later, when I comment on *The Four Ways of Knowing of an Awakened Person,* this is far from being so. Regrettably, some who have a shallow awakening and who then write and talk about it incessantly feed this misunderstanding. They eventually create a whole myth around the experience, which, because others wish to believe that magic and miracles are possible, is accepted as the truth. When a genuine teacher comes along who does not brag about his awakening and who behaves as an ordinary person, because he does not live up to the mythology, he is often rejected.

## HAKUIN AND ZEN MASTER SHOJU

Fortunately, Hakuin sought out an experienced teacher and told him what had happened. He also presented the teacher, Zen Master Shoju, with a verse, as was the custom. Shoju said, "This verse is what you have learned from study. Now show me what your intuition has to say," and he held out his right hand.

Hakuin replied, "If there were something intuitive that I could show you, I'd vomit it out," and he made a gagging sound.

The master asked, "How do you understand Joshu's *Mu?*" Hakuin replied, "What sort of place does *Mu* have that one can attach arms and legs to it?"

Master Shoju twisted his nose and said, "Here's somewhere to attach arms and legs." Hakuin did not know how to respond, and the master burst out laughing. "You poor hole-dwelling devil!" he cried. Hakuin ignored him, but the master continued, "Do you think somehow that you have sufficient understanding?"

Hakuin answered, "What do you think is missing?"

The master began to talk about the koan that tells of Zen master Nansen's death. Hakuin covered his ears with his hands and began to rush out of the room. On his way out, the master called to him, "Hey, monk!" and, after Hakuin had stopped and turned around, added, "You poor hole-dwelling devil!"

From then on, almost every time Hakuin went to the master he was called a "devil in the hole."[20]

One evening, the master sat cooling himself on the veranda. Hakuin took him another a verse he had written. "Delusions and fancies," the master said. Hakuin shouted his words back at him in a loud voice, whereupon the master grabbed him and beat him twenty or thirty times with his fists, and then pushed him off the veranda.

Hakuin says that this event happened "after a long spell of rain. I lay stretched out in the mud as though dead, scarcely breathing and almost unconscious. I could not move; meanwhile, the master sat on the veranda roaring with laughter. After a short while I regained consciousness, got up, and bowed to the master. My body was bathed in perspiration."

The master shouted after him, "You poor hole-dwelling devil!"[21]

After this Hakuin gave himself over, without stopping to sleep or eat, to a desperate practice based on the koan on the death of Nansen, which the master had given him. One day he had a slight awakening and went to the master's room to test his understanding, but the master would not approve it. All he did was call him "a poor hole-dwelling devil."

Hakuin began to think that he should leave his teacher and go elsewhere. One day he went to town to beg for food and met a madman who tried to hit him with a broom. Suddenly, Hakuin discovered that he had seen into the koan on the death of Nansen. Then he also saw into other koans that had puzzled him. He went back to Shoju and told him what he had seen and the understanding that he had gained. The master neither accepted nor rejected what he said, but only laughed pleasantly. However, from this time on, he stopped calling Hakuin a "poor hole-dwelling devil." Later, Hakuin experienced two or three further awakenings, accompanied by a great feeling of joy. "At times there are words to express such experiences," he writes, "But to my regret at other times there are none. It was as though I were walking about in the shadow cast by a lantern."[22]

One day Hakuin read a passage from the verse given by Kido Chigu to his disciple Nampo as they were parting: "As we go to part, a tall bamboo stands by the gate; its leaves stir the clear breeze for you in farewell." He was overcome with a great joy, as though a dark path had suddenly been illumined. Unconsciously he cried aloud, "Today for the first time I have entered the *samadhi* of words."[23] He arose and bowed in reverence.

This was not the end of Hakuin's journey into himself, but these few stories are enough to assess both the vigor of his practice and the depth of his realization. They also show the sincerity of his determination. How many people, after having had a spontaneous awakening, are prepared to seek someone to verify its authenticity? And how many would be prepared to accept the outlandish behavior offered in response by Shoju?

## HAKUIN'S WRITINGS

Books, letters, and writings of all kinds flowed out of Hakuin like lava from a volcano. All that he wrote underlined the vital importance of koan practice and, above all, of awakening. In this book, I will comment upon one of his most important texts: *The Four Ways of Knowing of an Awakened Person*. It is a fine introduction to the practice of Zen, but even more importantly, it has essential teachings for those who have practiced for a long while.

The practice of Zen is called *zazen*. *Za* means "sitting" and *zen*, which is a derivation of the Sanskrit word *dhyana*, means both "meditative absorption" and "beyond the opposites."[24] Zazen therefore means sitting beyond the opposites of "me" and the "world," "me" and "you," "me" and "God," and so on. Zazen can be seen to have three dimensions: meditation, concentration, and contemplation. To meditate is to allow the mind to circle some phrase, idea, or feeling. One does not try to understand the phrase, but instead allows understanding to come. Concentration means to focus one-pointedly upon a single thought or image. Contemplation means to be at one with whatever arises. Much of what Hakuin writes in *The Four Ways of Knowing of an Awakened Person* demands close contemplation.

*The Four Ways of Knowing of an Awakened Person* is little known in the West. It is, though, of great importance. I hope that this discussion of the text will help dispel some of the wrong ideas that prevail about awakening. Many believe that all spiritual experiences are the same, and that all religions ultimately have the same destination. This is not so. Spiritual life has an amazing diversity and has many levels and depths. I have shown why these differences exist in my book *Creating Consciousness*.[25] Let me nevertheless make a few comments now.

## ON THE DIVERSITY OF THE SPIRITUAL LIFE

There is a major distinction between practices that lead to *samadhi*, or absorption in meditative concentration, and practices that lead to awakening. As we have seen, Rinzai Zen emphasizes the latter. I quoted Hakuin earlier, describing his experience of awakening: "I chanced to hear the sound of the temple bell and I was suddenly transformed. It was as if a sheet of ice had been smashed, or a jade tower had fallen with a crash." All his former doubts "vanished as though ice had melted away." In contrast, a report in *Newsweek* gave the following account of a samadhi state:

> There was a feeling of energy centered in me . . . going out to infinite space and returning. . . . There was a relaxing of the dualistic mind, and an intense feeling of love. I felt a profound letting go of the boundaries around me, and a connection with some kind of energy and state of being that had a quality of clarity, transparency and joy. I felt a deep and profound sense of connection to everything, recognizing that there never was a true separation at all.[26]

These two accounts refer to vastly different situations. Samadhi is an *experience*, and has an incipient dualism embedded within it.[27]

Kensho is not an experience. With kensho, the *way* we experience is changed fundamentally. With kensho, the sleeping, creative intelligence is awakened, and at the same time the deeply engrained belief in the opposition between "the world" and "me" melts away. Because the age-old sense of separation dissolves, the anguish, despair, and fear that had accompanied it and had smoldered and burnt throughout life is also dissolved.

When Buddha first started his pilgrimage, he met three teachers. All three taught him meditation that led to samadhi. He eventually rejected these practices, although he became proficient in all three to the point that the teachers invited him to stay and become a teacher himself. Instead, he spent another six years undergoing spiritual trials before coming to awakening.

A distinction must also be made between zazen and meditation that leads to ecstatic states, visions, voices, and so on. One of the most famous of all Zen sayings is that of Rinzai Gigen, who said, "If you meet the Buddha, kill the Buddha!" In other words, any experience—even the most ineffable, whether of God, Jesus, or Buddha—is not your true nature, so do not get caught up with it.

Many people feel that the magical and miraculous are necessary in the spiritual life. Indeed, the Catholic Church will only beatify a person if evidence can be given that she or he was responsible for some magical or miraculous event. In Zen, such miraculous powers are not sought after; indeed, they are looked down upon. Zen master Dogen, for example, said that these kinds of powers come from bad karma. Also critical of miraculous powers, Zen master Hyakujo, while on a pilgrimage, met a fellow traveler with whom he walked for some distance. Eventually they came to a river and Hyakujo looked around for a ferry. His companion kept walking and called on Hyakujo to follow. Hyakujo, seeing the man walking on water, called, "You worthless good for nothing. If I had known that you were going to pull a trick like that, I would have left you hours ago!" And Layman P'ang, one of the more famous Zen laymen, wrote:

My miraculous power and magical activity,
Drawing water and carrying firewood.[28]

Even awakening is not homogenous and can be attained to
many different degrees and depths. This is surprising to many
Westerners, who believe that awakening necessarily is the same
for all. They usually exalt the person who has come to awakening as having achieved a kind of spiritually superior status.
When they hear of a person having more than one awakening,
they are dubious and wonder whether the original awakening
was genuine.

Hakuin ran up against the same kind of concerns when he
told his contemporaries that he had had many awakenings.
He laughed at the people who expressed such doubts, paro-
dying their concerns: "If you are enlightened, you are enlightened. If you are not, you are not. For a human being, the
severing of the life-root, which frees you from the clutches of
birth-and-death, is the single great matter. How can you count
the number of times it happens—as if it were a case of diar-
rhea?"[29] In other words, for these people, awakening was all
or nothing, not—as it was for Hakuin, and as it must be for
any true pilgrim—a major, indeed essential, step on the pilgrimage of spiritual life.

Life is a miracle. By this I mean that it is beyond all our
understanding, beyond all the laws of nature that we are able
to discern. It is spontaneous, creative, and without beginning
or end. But, we take life for granted. We even go so far as to
relegate it to being an accident, and say that it is the result of
some random occurrence, or we say that a living being is simply an elaborate machine driven by simple causal laws.

The truth will out. An old adage says that if you drive nature
out through the front door, she will return through the back

window. Although we take the miracle of *being* for granted, most people have a hunger for the magical, for the miraculous and divine. This means that if I cannot be miraculous, perhaps I can know the miraculous. Myths, rituals, superstitions, and religions have filled the void of our ignorance, our ignoring our true nature. Awakening is to awaken to the miracle of being, but those still shrouded in the mists of their own minds look outside for the miracle. Some look to the awakened person and expect him or her to manifest the miracle for them. But, as the Dhammapada says,

> By oneself evil is done;
> By oneself one suffers.
> By oneself evil is undone,
> No one can purify another.

We must do the work for ourselves. We cannot employ a vicar. Each of us must tread the path walking on our own feet. I hope that what follows will shed some light on the way, on practice and how practice can change the way we see the world. And I hope that it will help cut away some of the misconceptions about awakening.

# Introduction to the Text

_. . . ._

## Knowing, Knowledge, and Wisdom

IN _The Four Ways of Knowing of an Awakened Person,_ Hakuin describes the four ways of knowing, or four wisdoms, of the awakened mind. He quotes Zen master Shoju who speaks of these four as the Great Perfect Mirror Wisdom, the Universal Nature Wisdom, the Marvelous Observing Wisdom, and the Perfecting-of-Action Wisdom.

Thomas Cleary, in his translation of the title of this text, used the word _knowledge—The Four Knowledges._[1] The word _knowledge_—and this may be my own prejudice—seems to suggest something that is acquired. Knowledge also is usually based on thinking, and on thoughts arranged in a structure. As will be obvious, this is not what Hakuin had in mind. In other translations, for example, in Isshu Miura and Ruth Fuller Sasaki's _Zen Dust,_ the word _wisdom_ is used instead of knowing.[2] Wisdom is often used when translating the Sanskrit word _prajna,_ which is a key word in some of the sutras that Zen Buddhists prefer. The word _wisdom,_ however, has a variety of meanings.

The Sanskrit word _jnana_ is a cognate of the word _prajna,_ and is commonly translated as "knowledge," "wisdom," or "knowing." _Jnana_ and _prajna_ are essentially vital words. The best image of _prajna_ is the bodhisattva of wisdom Manjushri as he appears in Buddhist iconography. He is sometimes depicted seated on a lion, and most often he is shown wielding a sword. Manjushri is the incarnation, the personification, of *prajna*. The sword Manjushri wields is in motion; one should not see him as simply holding up the sword. Rather, Manjushri is in the process of swinging the sword, swirling it, moving it; the sword is in very rapid motion. *Prajna* is analogous to being by the sea and seeing the sun glinting off the waves. A continuous series of flashes shoot out: these are like the flash of *prajna*, the speed of *prajna*. This is why I say that *jnana* and *prajna* are essentially vital. When we think of wisdom, we tend to think of something that is acquired and that is static, a repository of wise sayings; very often we think of an old woman, or an old man with a beard, with a long history and rich experience to draw on. This is not in the way of *prajna*; *prajna* is the ability to respond spontaneously.

What is common to both *jnana* and *prajna* is *jna,* which is variously translated as "intelligence," "knowing," "awareness," or to be responsive and spontaneous. But this response is not a blind response, a knee-jerk response, or quick repartee.

*Jna* is basic to all life. For a long time now, our society has acquired the habit of looking on the origin of the world and of life as an accident, as a series of fortuitous comings-together, like blind logs bumping into each other in the night. More recently, a tendency to see that a remarkable intelligence or wisdom pervades all existence has been emerging. This wisdom not only pervades the conception and growth of the fetus and the embryo, but also continues with the healing of the body. When one cuts oneself, a spontaneous process occurs as the body heals this cut. Very often, not even a scar is left.

*Jna* is therefore fundamental; a fundamental wisdom or

knowing pervades the whole universe. This fundamental knowing sits in meditation. It works on the koans, indeed it wants to work on the koans, and it continues to do so even when all the clutter and noise of our lives seems to work so heavily against it. An intelligence persists, an intelligence or knowing that must have its way. This intelligence underlies the four ways of knowing and drives us on to their full realization. These four ways of knowing are simply four facets or faces of *jna*. In one sense, it truly doesn't matter if we have to live countless billions of lives to attain realization because the end is already complete, the goal has already been attained right here and now. Just lifting your hand, this is the end, this is the finality, the completeness. Of course, this finality, this end, this completeness is not an end in time or an ultimate attainment; it is the fulfillment of knowing, of *jna*. Realizing this gives us the basis for a secure faith in the practice. This faith is not faith in something that is beyond the clouds or beyond the heavens; this faith is in the working out of our everyday life through inherent knowing.

## KNOWING AND THE PRACTICE OF ZEN

The wisdom, knowing, or awareness that Hakuin speaks of in the *Four Ways of Knowing* is the very substance of Zen practice. When we search into a koan—for example, "Who am I?"—we are not searching in our experience to find a phenomenon that is "me"; we are not looking for that "thing" that is me. We are not looking for what we know, or for what we do not know; instead, we are looking into knowing itself. *What* I am is unimportant; *that* I am is all. This is the shift, the leap that we must make. A turnabout is necessary. Normally, we live within experience. We learn, we adapt, we shape our lives according to different experiences. We name what we experience, and in this way we build up a whole structure, a whole architecture—indeed, a whole mental city—in which we move around. This city of words, concepts, and relationships is what we normally call our lives, and we look upon ourselves as being "in" this life. Sometimes we look around and we call this city of concepts, structures, experiences, and habits "the world," and we believe that this is the only world. We are surprised when, for a moment, we encounter the world of another and find how different it is from our own. Most often, we feel that the other is mistaken, has misinterpreted experiences, does not understand, or is a "primitive," "heretic," or "foreigner." The insistence that my structure, my architecture, my plans, my words, my ways, my city is the only city is the cause of so many of our problems.

Let us change the metaphor for a moment. Each of us is acting a part in a play; we are also the director, star, stage manager, and audience of this play. We want—we *demand*—others to join in our play as extras; everyone wants everyone else to be extras in his or her play. Everyone says, "Come and play my game." Of course, a struggle, overt or covert, goes on because most people are not prepared to play a part in my theater, or if they will play a part, they want to be the star; but it is only me that can be the star.

When we are looking into "Who am I?," we are not looking into one of the characters, nor into one of the lines, nor into the shape or structure of the stage, nor of the theater, nor of the street in which the theater happens to be, nor of the country, the planet, nor even the galaxy. We are looking into that which knows, and that which knows is not a something. It cannot be found among other things.

## THE JUG AND THE CLAY

An analogy that masters often use is of a jug and the clay that it is made of. We are taken up with the shape of the jug, fascinated by it. The painting on the jug, the way that this jug fits in with a whole set of jugs, how it differs from other jugs, captivates our whole attention. We worry about whether it is more expensive or better than another's jug. I claim it is my jug and not your jug. We are so tied up in these aspects of the jug that we don't see the clay.

This clay is not only the clay of a jug, but it is also the clay of a cup, of a teapot, of an incense holder. This clay manifests in all kinds of ways, but generally it is ignored. Nobody goes around saying, "This is my clay."

The clay is a metaphor for knowing. We must be careful because, having said this, we have given knowing a form, a shape, and name. We call it *knowing, mind, awareness,* or *spirit.* Then we try to undo what we have done by saying it is *not mind* or *no-mind*; it is "not" spirit, "not" awareness. And so we thrash around like a serpent in a teapot. Nevertheless, somehow we have to point to this "whatever" if we are going to talk at all. But, we must not confuse the finger that points to the moon with the moon to which it points. None of our knowledge can ever lead us to knowing.

In koan number 28 of the classic koan collection the *Mumonkan*, Tokusan, after he came to awakening, sums up what I have just said: "Even though you have exhausted the abstruse doctrines, it is like placing a hair in vast space. Even though you have learned all the secrets of the world, it is like a drop of water dropped in the great ocean."[3]

When we think, or speak, about knowing or wisdom, we

should keep in mind their cosmic proportions. Wisdom is not simply a ragbag full of anecdotes, nor is it a blind impulsiveness. It is the dynamism of life, the dynamism of the cosmos, which is a wholeness, a oneness working in harmony. We shall refer to *knowing,* but knowing cannot be found anywhere. Knowing is not a substratum, and does not endure in time. We do not need to *be* something to know, nor to *know* something to be. Perhaps the best picture would be of a fountain, a fountain of life, light, and love.

## THE ORIGIN OF THE IDEA
## OF FOUR WAYS OF KNOWING

Asanga, the founder of the Yogacara, or "Consciousness-Only," school of Buddhism, was the first to introduce the idea that an awakened person has four ways of knowing. He called the first *mirror* knowing; the second is *universal* knowing, or knowing equality; the third he said was *observing* knowing (Hakuin calls this *differentiating* knowing); and the fourth he called the *perfection of action.* Asanga relates these four ways of knowing to the eight levels of consciousness.[4] The eighth level, *Alaya-vijnana,* he relates to the Great Mirror Knowing; he relates the the seventh level, *Manas,* to Universal Knowing; the sixth level to Observing Knowing; and the five senses to the Perfection of Action Knowing.[5]

By the ninth century, the Zen community had fully accepted what was called the "Yuishiki doctrine" of the relation between the three bodies of the Buddha (the *dharmakaya,* or dharma body; the *sambhogakaya,* or enjoyment body; and the *nirmanakaya,* or transformation body), the four ways of knowing, and the eight consciousnesses.[6] Zen master Daishu Ekai explains the connection between these:

The way of knowing called Great Perfect Mirror Wisdom alone makes the Dharmakaya; the way called Universal Nature Wisdom alone makes the Sambhogakaya; those called Marvelous Observing Wisdom and the Perfecting-of-Action Wisdom together make the Nirmanakaya. These three bodies are tentatively given names, and their differentiation in speech permits unenlightened persons to understand them. But once you have fully comprehended this principle, there will be no longer be three bodies responding to needs.[7]

The three Bodies of Buddha are quite esoteric, and we do not have to be too concerned with them here. Rinzai Gigen brings them down to earth by saying:

The pure light in your single thought—this is the Dharmakaya Buddha within your own house. The nondiscriminating light in your single thought—this is the Sambhogakaya Buddha within your own house. The nondifferentiating light in your single thought— this is the Nirmanakaya Buddha within your own house. This Threefold Body is you, listening to my discourse right now before my very eyes. . . .

According to the masters of the sutras and *shastras*, the Threefold Body is regarded as the ultimate norm, [as being absolute]. But in my view this is not so. This Threefold Body is merely a name; moreover, it is a threefold dependency. A man of old said: "The [Buddha] bodies are posited depending upon meaning, the [Buddha] lands are postulated in keeping with substance." Therefore we clearly know that

Dharma-natured bodies and Dharma-natured lands
are no more than reflections.[8]

## THE FOUR WAYS OF KNOWING
## AS FOUR WAYS OF ASKING, "WHO AM I?"

Although Hakuin writes about the four ways of knowing of
an awakened person, even if you are not awakened, you can
still benefit from what he has to say. The four ways of knowing can be looked upon as four ways of working on the question, "Who am I?"

The first of these ways is to use the question as a *hua t'ou.*
*Hua t'ou* is a Chinese word that literally means the "head of a
sentence." For example, instead of asking, "Who am I?" one
simply asks the question, "Who?" The rest of the question is
understood. By breathing "Who?" in and out, the question is
held steadily, and one can continue to practice for very long
periods. A variation of this same question is, "How do I know
that I am?" The only worthwhile response to both of these
questions is awakening. This awakening, as we shall see, is the
first way of knowing.

Another way of working on "Who am I?" is to ask, "When
a bird sings, where am I?" Or, "When it snows, where am I?"
The resolution of these questions is to awaken into the second way of knowing.

The third way of working on "Who am I" is to take all experience, no matter what, good or bad, pleasant or unpleasant,
and ask, "Who is experiencing this?" This will lead to the third
way of knowing.

The fourth way of working on "Who am I" is to inquire,
"Who walks?" "Who talks?" "Who eats?" "Who sits in zazen?"
This leads to awakening to the fourth way of knowing.

## LAY PRACTICE

Hakuin encouraged the layperson as well as the monk and nun to practice. Many of his letters that have been translated into English are written to laypeople engaged in the ordinary business of life. His writing on the four ways of knowing is just as relevant for a layperson as for a monk or nun.

One of the most frequent objections that laypeople have is that they do not have time to practice. In response to this, Hakuin said:

> Do not say that worldly affairs and pressures of business leave you no time to study Zen under a Master, and that the confusions of daily life make it difficult for you to continue your meditation. . . . Supposing a man accidentally drops two or three gold coins in a crowded street swarming with people. Does he forget about the money because all eyes are upon him? Does he stop looking for it because it will create a disturbance? Most people will push others out of the way, not resting until they get the money back into their own hands. Are not people who neglect the study of Zen because the press of mundane circumstances is too severe, or stop their meditation because they are troubled by worldly affairs, putting more value on two or three pieces of gold than on the unsurpassed mysterious way of the Buddhas? A person who concentrates solely on meditation amid the press and worries of everyday life will be like the man who has dropped the gold coins and devotes himself to seeking them. Who will not rejoice in such a person?[9]

Hakuin once wrote a letter to encourage a governor of one of the Japanese provinces. The governor obviously was a man who was immersed in the activities of everyday life, and Hakuin exhorted him to continue with his practice in the midst of his affairs. Hakuin said that the Hinayanists of old—Buddhists who relied upon the original sutras of Buddhism—are often looked down upon, although people of his day could not be compared with them in the meditation power, brilliance of insight, wisdom, and virtue that they had gained.[10] He explained that "it was only because the direction of their practice was bad, because they liked only places of solitude and quiet," that they "knew nothing of the dignity of the Bodhisattva" and were so reviled later and scorned by Vimalakirti, who looked upon them as "men who would scorch buds and cause seeds to rot."[11]

Hakuin also quoted the third patriarch, Sosan, who said that if you wish to awaken, then you must not avoid what the senses have to offer. However, this does not mean that you should indulge yourself in sense objects. Hakuin writes, "Just as the wings of a waterfowl do not get wet even when it enters the water, one must establish a mind that will continue a true koan meditation without interruption, neither clinging to nor rejecting the objects of the senses." Someone who fanatically avoids sense objects and dreads "the eight winds that stimulate the passions," Hakuin says, "unconsciously falls into the pit of the Hinayana and never will be able to achieve the Buddha Way."[12] The eight winds that stir the passions are winning and losing, backbiting, flattery, praise, humiliation, pain, and pleasure.

In another reply to laypeople who complain of the distractions of their lives, Hakuin quotes Zen master Yoka Genkaku, who said that the strength of mind gained by practicing meditation in the everyday world of desire and action "is like the lotus that rises from fire; it can never be destroyed. . . . When Yung-chia [Jap.: Yoka Genkaku] talks about the lotus in the midst of the flames, he is not simply referring the rare person in this world who practices Buddhism. What he is saying is that any place, no matter where, is the Zendo."[13]

Hakuin observed that even recluses who live in the forests or the desert, who eat just one meal a day and who practice the Way both night and day, still find it difficult to give themselves entirely to the practice. He went on to say:

> How much harder must it be then for one who lives with his wife and relatives amid the dusts and turmoils of this busy life? But if you do not have the eye to see into your own nature, you will not have the slightest chance of being responsive to the teaching. Therefore Bodhidharma has said: "If you wish to attain the Buddha Way, you must first see into your own nature."[14]

After coming to awakening, the sense objects themselves then will form the basis of practice. The five desires—possessions, sex, food, fame, and sleep—themselves will be the One Vehicle. In this way, speech and silence, activity and rest, all will be present in the midst of Zen meditation.

Hakuin continues the metaphor of the lotus, again to encourage the layperson to practice: "Because the lotus that blooms in the water withers when it comes near to fire, fire is the dread enemy of the lotus. Yet the lotus that blooms from the midst of flames becomes all the more beautiful and fragrant the nearer the fire rages."[15] To explain this metaphor, he says that if you practice by avoiding from the very beginning the five senses, it will not matter how deeply you penetrate the emptiness of self and things. No matter how much insight you may gain into the Way, you will be like a monkey with no tree to climb. When you leave behind the peace of solitude and go back into the world, you will lose all of your power. You will be like the lotus that withers at once when faced with the fire.

But if you go on courageously in the midst of your ordinary life, you will experience a great joy, as if suddenly you had made clear the basis of your own mind and had crushed the root of birth and death. Hakuin writes, "It will be as if the empty sky vanished and the iron mountain crumbled. You will be like the lotus blooming in the midst of the flames whose color and fragrance become more intense the nearer the fire approaches."[16] Why is this so? "Because the very fire is the lotus and the lotus is the fire."[17]

## NOTE ON THE LAYOUT OF THIS BOOK

In what follows, I will first present the whole of Hakuin's text as he wrote it, without comment. I will then repeat passages of the text in sections and make comments on each section. The reader has the option of reading the text and then the comments, or reading the comments and then the text. I have used this text for many *teishos* (dharma talks) that I have given to students during *sesshins* (Zen retreats) through the years of my teaching. My concerns have always been those of a teacher, and I have tried to portray the vigor and spirit with which the original was undoubtedly imbued. The text I present is based on various sources, including the excellent translation of Thomas Cleary.[18]

# The Four Ways of Knowing
## of an Awakened Person
.....

## HAKUIN'S TEXT

S OMEONE ASKED HAKUIN, "Are the three bodies and four
ways of knowing inherent, or are they brought into being
by our coming to awakening? Furthermore, are they realized
suddenly, all at once, or, with practice, do they come gradually?"

Hakuin answered by saying that although the three bodies[1]
and four ways of knowing are originally inherent and complete
in everyone, unless they are brought to light they cannot be
realized. After you have become strong through study and
practice, and the awakened nature suddenly manifests, you
realize the essence of inner reality all at once. When one way
of knowing is realized, all are realized. However, although you
reach the level of Buddhahood suddenly, and without passing
though steps and degrees, if you do not practice gradually, you
cannot reach pure, unobstructed knowing (*sarvajnata*)[2] and
ultimate great awakening.

## THE WAY OF KNOWING
## OF THE GREAT PERFECT MIRROR

Someone then asked, "What does realization all at once mean?"

Hakuin answered that when the discriminating mind is

suddenly shattered and the awakened essence immediately appears, the universe is filled with its boundless light. This is called the way of knowing of the Great Perfect Mirror, the pure body of reality (*dharmakaya*). This is realization all at once. At this time *alaya*, the eighth level of consciousness, is transmuted.

## THE WAY OF KNOWING EQUALITY

That all things in the six fields of sense—seeing, hearing, discernment, and knowledge—are your own awakened nature is called knowing equality, the fulfilled body of reward (*sambhogakaya*).

## THE WAY OF KNOWING BY DIFFERENTIATION

Discerning principles by the light of true awareness is the way of knowing by differentiation.

## THE WAY OF PERFECTION OF ACTION

Coughing, spitting, moving the arms, activity, stillness, all that is done in harmony with the nature of reality, is called knowing through doing things. This is the sphere of freedom of the transformation body (*nirmanakaya*).

Even so, you still do not see the way with complete clarity, and your power of shining insight is not yet fully mature. Therefore, if you do not go on with your practice, you will be like a merchant who hoards his capital and doesn't engage in trade. In this way, not only does he never become rich, but eventually he even goes broke through spending just to keep up the appearance of being wealthy.

What do I mean by going on with your practice? It is like a

merchant engaged in trade who spends a hundred dollars to make a profit of a thousand. In this way he accumulates vast wealth and treasure, and so becomes free to do as he will with his blessings. Whether rich or poor, money is still money, but without engaging in trade, it is impossible to get rich. Even if your breakthrough to reality is genuine, if your power of shining insight is weak, you cannot break down the barriers of habitual actions. Unless your knowing of differentiation is clear, you cannot benefit sentient beings according to their abilities. Therefore, you must know the essential road of gradual practice.

## GREAT FAITH, GREAT DOUBT

Hakuin then asks, rhetorically, "What is Great Perfect Mirror knowing?"

He replies that it means that if you want to see into this great matter, you must first generate great will, great faith, and great determination to see through the originally inherent, awakened nature.

After great will, faith, and determination are aroused, you should then constantly ask, "Who is the host of seeing and hearing?" Walking, standing, sitting, lying down, active or silent, whether in favorable or unfavorable circumstances, throw your mind into the question of what it is that sees everything here and now. What hears?

Question like this, ponder like this—ultimately, what is it? If you keep on doubting continuously, with a bold spirit and a feeling of shame urging you on, your effort will naturally become unified and solid, turning into a single mass of doubt throughout heaven and earth. The spirit will feel suffocated, the mind distressed, like a bird in a cage, like a rat that has gone into a bamboo tube and cannot escape.

At this time, if you just keep going without falling back, you will feel that you are entering a crystal world; the whole world, inside and outside, mats and ceiling, houses and cars, fields and mountains, grasses and trees, people and animals, utensils and goods, all are as they are but like illusions, like dreams, like shadows, like smoke. When you open your eyes clearly with presence of mind and see with certainty, an inconceivable realm appears that seems to exist, yet also seems not to exist in a way. This is called the time when the knowing essence becomes manifest.

## THE GATE OF INSPIRATION

If you think this is wonderful and extraordinary and joyfully become infatuated and attached to this, you will, after all, fall into the cave of demons and will never see the real, awakened nature.

At this point, if you do not fondly cling to your state but arouse your spirit to wholehearted effort, from time to time you will experience such things as forgetting you are sitting when you are sitting, forgetting about standing when you are standing, forgetting your own body, forgetting the world around you.

Then, if you keep going without retreating, the conscious spirit will suddenly shatter and the awakened nature will appear all at once. This is the Great Perfect Mirror knowing.

This is the first stage of inspiration; you can discern the source of eighty thousand doctrines,[3] with their limitless subtle meanings, all at once. As one becomes, all become; as one decays, all decay—nothing is lacking, no principle is not complete. As a newborn child of Buddha, the new bodhisattva will reveal the sun of wisdom of the awakened nature; but even so, the clouds of his former actions will not have yet been cleared away.

Because one's power in the way is weak and one's perception of reality is not perfectly clear, the Great Perfect Mirror wisdom is associated with the easterly direction and called the Gate of Inspiration. It is like the sun rising in the east—although the mountains, rivers, and land receive the sun's rays, they are not yet warmed by its light. Although you may have seen the way clearly, if your power of shining through is not strong enough, you may be blocked by inherent and chronic afflictions, and will still not be free and independent in both agreeable and adverse situations. This is like someone who has been looking for an ox and who may one day see through to the real ox, but if he doesn't hold the halter firmly to hold it in check, it will, sooner or later, run away.

Once you have seen the ox, make ox herding your only concern. Without this practice, after awakening, many people who have seen reality miss the boat. Therefore, to reach knowing of equality, do not linger in Great Perfect Mirror knowing. Go on and on, concentrate on practice after awakening.

## THE GATE OF PRACTICE

First, with the intimate perception, which you have had into knowing itself, enlighten all worlds with radiant insight.

When you see something, shine through it; when you hear, shine through what you are hearing; shine through the five *skandhas* (form, feeling, perception, will, consciousness); shine though the six fields of sense perception—in front, behind, left and right, through seven calamities and eight disasters, become one with radiant vision of the whole body. See through all things, internal and external; shine through them. When this work becomes solid, then perception of reality will be perfectly, distinctly clear, just like looking at the palm of you hand.

At this point, while increasing the use of this clear knowing and insight, if you enter awakening, then shine though awakening. If you get into agreeable circumstances, then shine through agreeable circumstances. If you fall into adverse situations, then shine through adverse situations. When greed or desire arise, shine though greed and desire; when hatred or anger arise, shine through hatred and anger; when you act out of ignorance, shine through ignorance. When the three poisons of hatred, greed, and ignorance are no more, and the mind is pure, shine through that pure mind. At all times, in all places, be it desires, senses, gain, loss, right, wrong, visions of Buddha or of dharma, in all things shine through with your whole body.

If you do not fall back, the karma created by your former actions will dissolve naturally. You will be liberated in a way that cannot be imagined.

The way you act will conform to how you understand. Host and guest will merge completely. Body and mind will no longer be two, and what you are and the way you appear will not obstruct each other. Getting to the state of true equanimity is called knowing equality as the nature of reality.

This way of knowing is associated with the southerly direction and called the Gate of Practice. It is like when the sun is in the south, its light is full and brings light to all the hidden places in the deep valleys, melting even the most solid ice and drying the ground however wet. Although a bodhisattva has the eye to see reality (kensho), unless you go through this gate of practice, you cannot clear away obstructions brought about by afflictions and actions and therefore cannot attain to the state of liberation and freedom. What a pity that would be, what a loss.

## THE GATE OF AWAKENING

After you have reached the nondual realm of equality of reality, it is essential that you then clearly understand the awakened ones' profound principle of differentiation. After this you must master the methods for helping sentient beings. Otherwise, even though you have developed and attained unhindered knowing, you will, nevertheless, remain in the nest of the Hinayana and will be unable to realize total, unobstructed knowing. You will lack freedom to change in any required way to help sentient beings, to awaken yourself and others, and reach the ultimate Great Awakening where awareness and action are completely perfect.

This is why one must arouse an attitude of deep compassion and commitment to help all sentient beings everywhere.

To begin with, you should study day and night the verbal teachings of the Buddha and patriarchs so that you can penetrate the principles of things in their infinite variety. Ascertain and analyze, one by one, the profundities of the five houses and the seven schools of Zen and the wondrous doctrines of the eight teachings given in the five periods of Buddha's teaching career.

If you have any energy left over, you should clarify the deep principles of the various different philosophies. However, if this and that get to be too much trouble, it will just waste your energy to no avail. If you thoroughly investigate the sayings of the Buddhas and patriarchs that are difficult to pass through, and clearly arrive at their essential meaning, perfect understanding will shine forth and the principles of all things should naturally be completely clear. This is called the eye to read the sutras.

Now, the verbal teachings of the Buddhas and the patriarchs

are extremely deep, and one should not consider that one has mastered them completely after one has gone through them once or twice. When you climb a mountain, the higher you climb, the higher they are; when you go into the ocean, the farther you go, the deeper it is. It is the same in this case. It is also like forging iron to make a sword; it is considered best to put it into the forge over and over, refining it again and again. Though it is always the same forge, unless you put the sword in over and over and refine it a hundred times, it can hardly turn out to be a fine sword.

Penetrating study is also like this; unless you enter the great forge of the Buddha and patriarchs, difficult to pass through, and make repeated efforts at refinement, through suffering and pain, total and independent knowing cannot come forth. Penetrating through the barriers of the Buddha and patriarchs over and over again, responding to beings' potential everywhere with mastery and freedom of technique, is called subtle, observing, discerning knowing.

You do not investigate by means of intellectual considerations. This way of knowing, to save yourself and to liberate others, when completely fulfilled and mastered, is subtle, observing, discerning knowing. This is the state of the perfectly fulfilled body of reward; it is associated with the westerly direction and called the Gate of Awakening. It is like the sun having passed the high noon, gradually sinking toward the west. While the great way of knowing of equality is right in the middle, the faculties of sentient beings cannot be seen and the teachings of differentiation among things cannot be made clear. If you do not stop in the realm of self-enlightenment as inner realization but, instead, cultivate this subtle, observing, discerning knowing, you have done what you can do; having done your task, you can reach the land of rest. This rest is not what the setting sun means; it means that you have accomplished all the ways of knowing, have fulfilled awakening, because awakening self and others, fulfillment of awareness and action, is considered real ultimate awakening.

## THE GATE OF NIRVANA

This is the secret gateway to the command of the mind and is the realm of ultimate liberation. This is knowing without any kind of defilement, a virtue that is not created. If you do not realize this way of knowing, you will not be able to do freely what must be done to benefit yourself and others. It is the effortless way.

Because the preceding way of knowing by differentiation is gained through correct practice, it is in the realm of cultivation: realization is gained by practice. It is therefore a way of knowing that is reached through effort. The way of knowing perfect action transcends the bounds of practice, realization, and attainment through study. It is beyond any kind of demonstration or explanation. One could say that knowing by way of differentiation is like the flower of complete awakening; practice is this flower coming into bloom. On the other hand, with knowing and "doing what needs to be done," the flower of full awakening and practice drops away and the fruit ripens. You cannot possibly see this even in a dream unless you have passed through the final stages of transcendence of our school. That is why it is said that at the last word, you finally come to the impenetrable barrier.

The way to point out the direction is not in verbal explanations; if you want to reach this realm, just refine your subtle, discerning knowing through the differentiating and difficult-to-pass-through koans, smelting and forging hundreds of times, over and over. Even if you have passed through some, repeat them over and over, examining meticulously—what is this little truth beyond all convention in the great matter of transcendence? If you do not regress in your examination of the sayings of the ancients, someday you may come to know this bit of wonder.

Even so, if you do not seek an awakened master and personally enter his forge, you cannot plumb the profound subtleties. The only worry is that real teachers of Zen are extremely few and hard to find. But if someone exerts his energy to the utmost in this, and penetrates through clearly, he attains freedom in all ways, transcends the realms of Buddhas and devils, resolves sticking points, removes bonds, pulls out nails and pegs, and leads people to the realm of purity and ease. This is called the knowing required to accomplish works. It is associated with the northerly direction and is called the Gate of Nirvana. It is like when the sun reaches the northern quarter, when it is midnight and the whole world is dark; reaching the sphere of this knowing is not within understanding or comprehension—even Buddhas can't see, much less outsiders and devils.

This is the thoroughly peaceful state of pure reality of the Buddhas and patriarchs, the forest of thorns that patch-robed monks sit, lie, and walk in twenty-four hours a day. This is called great nirvana, replete with four attributes (self, purity, bliss, and eternity). It is also called knowing the essential nature of the cosmos, in which the four ways of knowing are fully complete. The center means harmonizing the four ways of knowing into a whole, and the essential nature of the cosmos means the king of awakening, master of the teachings, being king of the dharma, free in all ways.

I hope that you Buddhists of great faith will arouse great trust and commitment and develop the great practice for the realization of these four ways of knowing and true awakening.

Do not forgo the great matter of countless ages just because of pride in your present view.

# COMMENTARY ON
## *The Four Ways of Knowing of an Awakened Person*

L ET US NOW RETURN to Hakuin and the four ways of knowing and the three bodies of the Buddha. Hakuin taught tirelessly the truth that practice is essential if one is to realize all four ways of knowing. He says elsewhere, "Followers of the Way, even though you may have pursued your studies in the Threefold Learning continuously through many *kalpas* [aeons], if you have not directly experienced the Four Wisdoms, you are not permitted to call yourselves true sons of Buddha."[1]

## ARE THE THREE BODIES INHERENT?

Someone asked Hakuin, "Are the three bodies and four ways of knowing inherent, or are they brought into being by our coming to awakening? Furthermore, are they realized suddenly, all at once, or, with practice, do they come gradually?"

Hakuin answered by saying that although the three bodies and four ways of knowing are originally inherent and complete in everyone, unless they are

brought to light they cannot be realized. After you
have become strong through study and practice, and
the awakened nature suddenly manifests, you realize
the essence of inner reality all at once. When one way
of knowing is realized, all are realized. However,
although you reach the level of Buddhahood suddenly,
and without passing though steps and degrees,
if you do not practice gradually, you cannot reach
pure, unobstructed knowing (*sarvajnata*) and
ultimate great awakening.

### the three bodies and four ways of knowing are originally inherent and complete in everyone

All of us, inherently, have, or, more precisely *are*, these four
ways of knowing. Furthermore, they are not separate and dis-
tinct ways of knowing, but are different ways our fundamental, true nature manifests. They are different perspectives. An
analogy would be the plan, side elevation, front elevation, and
three-quarter elevation of a building that architectural drafts-
men draw. Each of these refers to the same building, but seen
from different viewpoints. In the same way, these ways of
knowing and the three bodies are all looking at the same bril-
liant diamond: the scintillating self-nature.

### unless they are brought to light they cannot be realized

The basic sin of Buddhism is ignorance. Buddhists use the
word *klesha* instead of sin, and *klesha* is most often translated
as "defilement" or "aberration." With the word *ignorance,* the
Buddhist does not refer to a lack of knowledge or education.
Ignorance means that we ignore, or turn our back on, our true

nature, which is whole and complete. Our natural state is samadhi, a unity that is a seamless whole.[2] Although we turn our back on it, that does not mean that true nature ceases to exist. However, we must "turn around" to realize that this is so. This turnabout is called *paravritti, satori,* or *kensho.* We normally use the word *kensho* to refer to our first awakening to the truth that we are whole and complete. Inherently we have all that is necessary for a life of love, wisdom, and happiness. Our dualistic view hides this truth from us. Kensho is the first intimation that dualism, which makes us feel divided against others, the world, and ourselves, and therefore causes us to suffer, is indeed an illusion. Ultimately, this turnabout, when it is complete, is what Hakuin means by "bringing the four ways of knowing to light."

**After you have become strong through study and practice, and the awakened nature suddenly manifests, you realize the essence of inner reality all at once.**

Awakening comes all at once; this is why it is sudden. We must not confuse sudden awakening with instant awakening. Instant coffee is coffee that we make without the grinding and percolating. However, even with sudden awakening, the grinding and percolating are still necessary. Suddenness is the mark of authentic awakening; awakening has an explosive quality about it. Suppose you're working on a puzzle or a problem and then, suddenly, you see the solution. "Ah yes!" It comes all at once. A very famous story is told of the mathematician Henri Poincaré. He had struggled for a long time trying to resolve a particularly difficult mathematical problem. He went on an excursion one day and forgot about the problem. Then suddenly, as he stepped on the bus, all at once the whole solution was presented to him. This all-at-once character gives the shock, the shattering quality of kensho.

Awakening is sudden not only because it appears without warning, but also because it does not endure as an experience. Because it is not an experience, it has no temporal component. Awakening is not an experience; it is a change in the *way* we experience. Many people confuse an experience of unity and completeness with awakening. This is why we must have an awakening authenticated by a teacher. Any experience—even the most intense, meaningful, and transformative—is not awakening. I am not putting this kind of experience down, but it is important to make the distinction. Because awakening is sudden and without warning, we cannot, as a rule, prejudge it or anticipate it. We cannot say, "I'm getting near" or "I'm not near," or ask, "When we will I get near?" This is why a master will tell us that we cannot judge our own practice. A so-called unconscious aspect of our practice, as well as the conscious sense of practicing, are vital to realization. This is obvious in the example of Poincaré. Although the resolution to his problem was sudden, instantaneous, and complete, nevertheless the conscious struggle that he had undertaken during the preceding months was essential. And so was the "unconscious" work that preceded the arrival of the resolution.

How often have you struggled to remember the name of someone, only to give it up, and then find, several days later, after you had even forgotten about trying to remember the name, that it suddenly appears? This must mean that, at some level, the work of remembering the name had gone on continuously. The conscious striving was necessary, but only so that this deeper level could take over and finish the work. This is how it is with the practice of Zen. When we realize that both conscious and unconscious work are necessary, we can have deep faith in our practice, even when we feel that nothing seems to be happening. We can have deep faith that this latent work is indeed being done.

We should also realize when considering sudden awakening that, as Hakuin says elsewhere, "When one thing is realized, all is realized." It's as a master said, "If you see through a speck of dust, you see through the whole world!" People sometimes challenge me, saying, "You know, the problems of the world are so great, and my own particular problems are so many, I just don't understand how we can waste our time just asking this single question, 'Who am I?' Surely much more must be involved in true spiritual work than just asking one question ceaselessly in this way." This doubt seems to become even more pressing as the one question becomes dry and dead and without interest. What about all these other problems? Why don't we do something about them? To see into this one question is to see into them all. As Zen master Daie Soko said, "Go for the root, never mind about the branches, leaves, flowers, and fruit! Cut the root!"

**although you reach the level of Buddhahood suddenly, . . . if you do not practice gradually, you cannot reach pure, unobstructed knowing (*sarvajnata*) and ultimate great awakening.**

This means that though sudden awakening may occur, nevertheless, at that time, a new, gradual practice begins, which steadily unveils what one has awakened to. It's like a person who has been blind from birth and whose eyes are operated upon and is given sight. Initially, when he begins to see, he just sees blazing light. Furthermore, this experience is often very painful. During a long while after the operation, he has to painfully reconstruct his world, while undoing the world that he had created while blind. Because the work is so arduous, some people who have this kind of operation wish that they had remained blind.

After working through the first, breakthrough, koan, we work through many other koans. Each of these subsequent koans, in its own way, is a breakthrough koan; each brings a new kensho and has its own "Aha!" connected with it. Although any koan that we work with can be a breakthrough koan, it happens that some are easier to work with in this way.[3] If our work on a koan does not bring about this "Aha!"—even though it may not be an explosive "Aha!"—we can be sure we have not seen into it. This means that although practice is gradual, it is not continuous or linear, but progresses by discrete leaps.

The "Aha!" of insight comes when we create. We cannot use the logical mind to create but must rely on a deeper mind. We rely upon this same deeper mind to work on koans, because the response to a koan is not logical, as we understand that term. If we give a logical answer, we have used the discriminating mind, the mind of either/or and yes and no, to find it. In other words, having a bag of responses to koans is quite useless if these responses do not come from a creative response, and so do not help to widen and deepen the breach that was made with our initial awakening.

Those still working in the dark often misunderstand awakening. They hear that somebody is awakened and they are immediately looking for a saint, looking for some superior kind of being with light flaming out of her ears and glaring eyes, and with the wisdom of the ages in her pocket. It is not like that at all, fortunately.

In the *Diamond Sutra*, Buddha has the following conversation with Subhuti. He asks, "Can the Tathagata [this term was used by Buddha when referring to himself] be recognized by some material characteristic?"

Subhuti replies, "No, World-Honored One; the Tathagata cannot be recognized by any material characteristic. Why? Because the Tathagata has said that material characteristics are not in fact material characteristics. Wherever there are material characteristics there is delusion; but whoso perceives that all characteristics are in fact no-characteristics perceives the Tathagata."[4] An awakened person cannot be recognized by any outward sign or manifestation, even after that person has undergone years of patient, gradual practice after awakening. As Hakuin says, "You will still be the same old monk you always were. You won't be doing anything out of the ordinary. Your eyes will stare out from your face from the same location as before. Your nose will be where it always was."[5]

On the one hand, Hakuin says that awakening is something wonderful: "Now you will be the genuine article, an authentic descendant of the Buddhas and patriarchs, to whom you will have fully repaid that incalculable debt of gratitude which you owe them."[6] Awakening is truly most wonderful. Nothing can compare with that moment when one truly sees into one's true nature and the world turns upside down. Nothing! It's incomparable. On the other hand, Hakuin says it isn't very much.

Awakening means, fundamentally, that we can now work in a way that beforehand was very difficult. Nevertheless, the work has to be done. Even though we may still be working in the dark, and we realize awakening is vital, we must not wait for awakening before doing our spiritual work. Zen says that some people work and come to awakening, other people awaken and then they work. But the work has to be done.

Very often, people who come to spontaneous awakening

outside a tradition, because they do not undertake this work after awakening, become distorted and weird at best. Very often they become prophets and gurus and spread their own subjective ideas. They can be very dangerous people because a certain charisma comes with the awakened state, arising out of complete faith, and yet this charisma can be misguided and mixed with all kinds of strange ideas and practices. To quote Hakuin once more: "If . . . you follow the trend of the times, when you enter the dark cave of unknowing in the eighth consciousness, you will start bragging about what you have achieved. You will go around telling everyone how enlightened you are. You will accept, under false pretenses, the veneration and charity of others, and wind up being one of those arrogant creatures who declares he has attained realization when he has not." [7]

Whether you are awakened or not, working on the koan "Who am I?" and painfully and painstakingly continuing to question, to probe, to search, to ask, is never wasted work. After awakening, our character must be refined. But, this refinement of the character comes by itself to anyone, awakened or not, who is truly sincere and working not for any self-glory or self-gain, but simply because of that sense of the religious life, of the true life, of the worthwhile life. By accepting that this is so, we can work out of the faith that this practice is intrinsically worthwhile. The practice then comes from the feeling of the holy, the sense of the whole, the sense of the rightness of what we are doing; we practice because it is right and not because of what we can get out of the practice.

This attitude to practice is itself of immeasurable importance. It is a call to have true faith in oneself and in one's practice. The very intuition that we have of the rightness of what we're doing is itself very valuable. People once upon a time talked in terms of conscience. We never hear the word *conscience* anymore, do we? But what I am talking about is working according to our conscience.

## GREAT PERFECT MIRROR KNOWING

**Someone then asked, "What does realization all at once mean?"**
**Hakuin answered that when the discriminating mind is suddenly shattered and the awakened essence immediately appears, the universe is filled with its boundless light. This is called the way of knowing of the Great Perfect Mirror, the pure body of reality (*dharmakaya*). This is realization all at once. At this time *alaya*, the eighth level of consciousness, is transmuted.**

Let us take this paragraph step by step.

**when the discriminating mind is suddenly shattered**

It sounds very violent to say that the discriminating mind "suddenly shatters." Someone heaves a brick at a shop window, and the window is shattered into a thousand pieces. One cannot quite help wondering whether one wants the mind shattered in quite that way. Most of us do not want to shatter the discriminating mind because we feel that if we were to do so, we would end up gibbering in the corner. We need the discriminating mind in order to work, to do our daily tasks and chores, to understand what is going on around us, and to make judgments about the best course of action. Therefore, we should understand clearly what is meant by "when the discriminating mind is suddenly shattered."

When someone tells you a joke, if it is a good joke, you listen, all serious, and then all of a sudden, you just burst out laughing. Your mind is shattered for the moment. When you burst out laughing like that, everything is gone; one has nothing to hold on to at all.

A young man on vacation calls home and speaks to his brother, "How's Oscar the cat?"

"The cat's dead, died this morning."

"That's terrible. You know how attached I was to him. Couldn't you have broken the news more gently?"

"How?"

"You could've said that he's on the roof. Then, the next time I called, you could have said that you haven't been able to get him down, and gradually like this, you could've broken the news."

"Okay, I see. Sorry."

"Anyway, how's Mom?"

"She's on the roof."

If you reflect back on this, or on another joke that you have enjoyed, you will know the sudden breakup of the field of consciousness at the moment that you see into the joke. We use the expressions "It broke me up" or "I cracked up," meaning it was very funny. Hakuin is referring to this kind of shattering.

Laughter and awakening, furthermore, are very close relatives.

A monk went to visit Zen master Baso and asked, "What is the meaning of Bodhidharma's coming from the West?"

Baso said, "Bow down!"

As soon as the monk went down to bow, Baso kicked him. The monk had a great awakening. He rose up clapping his hands, and laughing heartily, said, "Wonderful! Wonderful! The source of myriad samadhis and limitless subtle meanings can all be realized on the tip of a single hair." He then paid his respects to Baso and withdrew.

Later, he told the assembly, "Since the day I was kicked by Master Baso, I have not stopped laughing."

When the discriminating mind is shattered, paradoxically, it does not break into pieces, but becomes suddenly one seamless whole. The shattering, sometimes called an explosion, occurs through a sudden release of tension through the arrival of unity. A bursting open irrupts, but at the same time, fulfillment is complete. Everything is fulfilled that before was held in restraint, in anxious equilibrium. The mind suddenly opens up, irrupts, so to speak. But it is not a destructive irruption. It is the irruption of a flower coming into bloom. If you have seen films of flowers coming into bloom in which the sequence has been speeded up, you will know what I mean by saying that a flower irrupts into bloom. Hakuin is referring to this kind of irruption or breaking open, the laughter of a flower as it explodes into bloom.

When the discriminating mind is suddenly shattered, it is shattered in a cosmic laugh, and "the awakened essence suddenly appears." The shattering of the discriminating mind and the appearance of the awakened essence are not two. The appearance of the awakened essence is the fulfillment aspect; the flower comes into bloom.

**the universe is filled with its boundless light.**

The universe is not filled with boundless light; the universe is already boundless light, but we suddenly come upon this truth, that the universe is boundless awareness, boundless light. And we feel, "Oh, it is filled with boundless light." But, as you sit there at this moment, the universe is, or is filled with, boundless light. Zen master Chosha said, "The entire world is your divine light." This is not a new state. Zen master Mumon calls this sudden transition *mumonkan,* the "gateless gate." It is called the gateless gate because undoubtedly, with kensho you pass through a gate, but no gate is there to pass through. When this boundless light suddenly makes itself known, a transition occurs, but the transition is not a step in time, it is waking up.

The boundless light is not a light that we can see, but the light *by which we see.* In the unawakened state we ignore this light. This is what Buddhism means by the *klesha* of ignorance. Jesus said that we are the light of the world. In the *Bhagavad Gita* it says, "He is the Light of lights, said to be beyond darkness. Knowledge, the object of knowledge, and the goal of knowledge—He is seated in the hearts of hearts. As the light of lights, it is from me that the sun, moon, and stars get their light; but I seek myself in shadows."[8] Rinzai Gigen, when talking about this light, said:

> Followers of the Way, mind is without form and pervades the ten directions.
>
> > In the eye it is called seeing,
> > In the ear it is called hearing.
> > In the nose it smells odors,
> > In the mouth it holds converse.
> > In the hands it grasps and seizes,
> > In the feet it runs and carries.
>
> Fundamentally it is one pure radiance; divided it becomes the six harmoniously united spheres of sense. Since the mind is nonexistent, wherever you are, you are emancipated.[9]

In koan number 86 of the *Hekigan-roku* (*Blue Cliff Record*), a collection of a hundred koans compiled by Zen master Setcho in the eleventh century, Ummon spoke of this light to the assembly, saying, "Everyone has his own light shining continuously now as of old. It cannot be seen or known. If he tries to see it, everything is darkness. What is your light?" Then, answering for the community, he said, "The kitchen pantry and the gate."

**the pure body of reality (*dharmakaya*)**

The word *kaya* in Sanskrit means "body." *Dharmakaya* means the body of dharma. Nisargadatta, the contemporary Hindu sage who died quite recently, said, "My body is peace and silence." My body: peace-and-silence-*kaya*. When Emperor Wu, in the first koan of the *Blue Cliff Record,* asked Bodhidharma what was his teaching, Bodhidharma replied, "Vast emptiness, not a thing that can be called holy." He could have said, "The *dharmakaya*."

The *dharmakaya* is empty because it has no content; it is vast because it has no boundary, no limit. Because it is empty, it is dark. As Ummon has just said, "If one tries to see it, everything is darkness." Hakuin says, "Followers of the Way, if your investigation has been correct and complete, at the moment you smash open the dark cave of the eighth, or *alaya,* consciousness, the precious light of the Great Perfect Mirror wisdom instantly shines forth. But, strange to say, the light of the Great Perfect Mirror wisdom is black like lacquer."[10]

The *Prajnaparamita Sutra,* a basic sutra in Zen, has its origin in the samadhi of the Great Perfect Mirror wisdom, or *dharmakaya.*[11] To truly appreciate the *Prajnaparamita Sutra,* one must see it from samadhi, that is to say, one should be in samadhi to chant it. The *Prajnaparamita* extols the world of the *dharmakaya,* the body (*kaya*) of the teaching (dharma). And the body of the teaching, this *dharmakaya,* is original samadhi, or true nature.

An analogy that I sometimes use to help people understand that we are always in samadhi is the following: Suppose you have a glass of pure water and you drop a little blue ink in the water; the ink is then suspended in the clear water. The ink obviously isn't the water, and the water isn't the ink. They are nevertheless inseparable. Everything—life, death, you, me, the world, good and bad—these are like the ink; all are suspended in the pure water of the samadhi of true nature, the *dharmakaya.*

In Zen, a traditional way to talk about awakening and what it involves is a series of ten pictures called the "ox-herding pictures." The first picture shows a little boy, the herdsman, running around looking for his ox. Each successive picture shows a gradual deepening of the awakened mind. The last three are concerned respectively with the *dharmakaya,* the *nirmanakaya,* and the *sambhogakaya.* A verse accompanies each of the pictures. The verse for picture number eight, the one referring to the *dharmakaya,* reads:

> Whip and rein, herdsman and ox, all have gone
> without leaving a trace.
> The vast, blue sky, how can words size it up?
> How can snow endure in the crimson flame of
> the burning fire?
> If you would stand eyeball to eyeball with the
> old masters,
> Here must you stand!

Shame! I used to wish to save the whole world.
What a shock. No world exists for me to save.
Words cannot be used to talk about
The herdsman in this realm.
Teacher, student both are no more.
Mystery of mysteries! Who is there to receive this truth?
Who is there to give it?

With one blow the vast sky is suddenly shattered.
Holy, profane, both are gone without trace.
In the pathless, all paths come to an end.
Brightly shines the moon; softly the wind rustles
In the courtyard of the temple.
The water of all the rivers flows into the great sea.

## the pure body of reality

The "emptiness" of the *dharmakaya* is not a huge cosmic hole. We are actually seeing the world in samadhi at this very moment. Zen master Kanzan, describing samadhi, says, "One day, after having my gruel, I took a walk. Suddenly I stood still, filled with the realization that I had no body or mind. All I could see was one great illuminating Whole—omnipresent, perfect, lucid, and serene. It was like an all-embracing mirror from which the mountains and rivers of the earth were projected as reflections."[12]

We overlook the fact that we *know* this world. We ignore the truth that the world is as it is because we *know* it to be so. When we say, "The sun is shining," or "The cat wants to go out," or "Breakfast is ready," we should say, "I know that . . ." before each statement. But to say, "I know that . . ." would be redundant. It goes without saying. Although saying "I know that . . ." is redundant, we must not infer that *knowing itself* is redundant. When we awaken we find that knowing is, and has always been, like an all-embracing mirror from which the mountains and rivers, the zendo and cushions, are projected as reflections.

Because we overlook knowing, which is the essence of "I know," we are just left with "I" and feel separated from ourselves, alienated, lost. The sun, the cat, breakfast, mountains, and rivers therefore seem separate from us, having their own independent existence. We then seek ourselves in the mountains and rivers, in the cushions and zendo; in short, we seek ourselves in experience.

When the world is seen in the Way of the Great Perfect Mirror, everything is suspended in knowing. No "knower" is necessary or possible; no viewpoint view exists from which all is seen. The seeing of it is the being of it. When someone asked Joshu, "What is Buddha?" (the question could just as well have been, "What is the *dharmakaya*?") Joshu said, "The oak tree in the garden." The seeing of the oak tree is the being of the oak tree. But this doesn't mean that the oak tree is simply the projection of some imagination.

What I am saying is not the same as what the idealist philosopher Bishop Berkeley said. According to the bishop, the tree is God's idea. For Joshu, neither God nor an idea arose. When I say, "seeing is being," I am not saying that seeing and being are the same. Seeing and being are not the same, but they cannot be separated, and so they are not different. Being is being and seeing is seeing, but being is seeing. In the *Prajna-paramita* it says, "Form is emptiness." Form is form; emptiness is emptiness. These are not the same, identical, but they are not two. Zen is neither monism nor dualism. To see into this is to see into the Great Perfect Mirror wisdom.

No seer exists either; no one sees. We insert the seer after the fact. The painter is part of the painting. Our immediate experience is the oak tree in the garden; this is this suspended mirror and its reflections. A Zen master asked a monk, "Is it the weather that is cold, or is it the man who feels the cold?" The monk replied, "We are all here!" Inside, outside, coming, going, all contained in samadhi: "We are all here." Or, as Hakuin says in his *Chant in Praise of Zazen,* coming and going, we never leave home. With kensho, we shatter the projection that a seer and a seen, a man who feels the cold and the weather that is cold, are the way things are, rather than they way they are thought to be. We shatter the illusion of a real, independently existing world as well as a permanently abiding subject. A haiku by Basho reads:

No one
Walks along this path
This autumn evening.

**This is realization all at once. At this time *alaya*, the eighth level of consciousness, is transmuted.**

Awakening is a turnabout or a turning around (*paravritti*), a turning around in the eighth storehouse consciousness (*alaya*)[13] and the emergence of the way of knowing called the Great Perfect Mirror. Awakening is not an idea, a thought, nor a different way of thinking. It is not an experience. Nor is it something new that has entered the mind. The mind itself has been turned over in a very fundamental way. One could even say that it has been turned inside out, something like a glove might be turned inside out. The glove is still the same glove, but it is quite different. This turning about, this turning over, requires great effort, great energy. This is the work that has to be done.

When I say that the work requires great energy, I do not mean that it is the work of pistons; it is not a thump-thump kind of work. We can thrash around like a thrashing machine and yet not be working. The work is penetrating, subtle, sincere work, but nevertheless it is work. A certain kind of exertion is necessary, and in our heart of hearts each of us knows what this exertion is—and each of us would rather run a mile than make this exertion. Dogen writes of it. He says that exertion is neither self-imposed nor imposed by others, but free and uncoerced. Later in the same article, he says that everything is exertion. Even to attempt to avoid exertion cannot be done, because the attempt itself is exertion. He writes, "This sustained exertion is not something which people of the world naturally love or desire, yet it is the last refuge of all."

Without exertion, no turnabout is possible. The extent of the turnabout is dependent upon the work that we do. If we do a little work, a little turnabout occurs; if we do intense work, a great turnabout occurs; if we do no work, no turnabout occurs. What we have to do is bring ourselves constantly back to the center of this work.

## KNOWING EQUALITY

**That all things in the six fields of sense—seeing, hearing, discernment, and knowledge—are your own awakened nature is called knowing equality, the fulfilled body of reward (*sambhogakaya*).**

The reward body is called the *sambhogakaya*, sometimes known as the "bliss body." It is said that Buddha reveals himself to the bodhisattvas through the *sambhogakaya* (that is, when the bodhisattva comes to awakening). What does all this mean in terms of our practice? This awakening comes as another turnabout, this time in the seventh level of consciousness, the *manas*. This way of knowing transcends duality. In experience, the first turnabout in the eighth consciousness opens onto knowing as emptiness, knowing as vast space. Many koans point to this; one example is the Bodhidharma's "Vast space, nothing to be called holy." Another is the second half of Nansen's "Everyday Mind Is the Way": "It is like vast space."[14] This is knowing as emptiness; it is seeing that form is emptiness. Many people, as Hakuin points out, are content to stay with this awakening. He attained to this level with his first kensho, but was fortunate to find a teacher who pushed him further. His teacher used to call him a "devil in the hole." The hole was Hakuin's awakening to the *dharmakaya*. The devil was Hakuin's willingness to stay there.

The need to go beyond the way of knowing of the Great Perfect Mirror is also emphasized in many koans. For example, in koan number 46 of the *Mumonkan*, Zen master Sekiso asked, "How will you step from the top of a hundred-foot pole?" And another eminent master of old said, "You, who sit on the top of a hundred-foot pole, although you have come to realization, you are not yet real. Go forward from the top of the pole and you will manifest your whole body in the ten directions." Manifesting your whole body in the ten directions is this second awakening. It is seeing that all things in the six fields of sense—seeing, hearing, discernment, and knowledge—are your own awakened nature.

This second awakening is deeper and more penetrating, and one sees that "all is one." Joshu's "Oak Tree in the Garden" and koan number 53 of the *Hekigan-roku*, "Hyakujo and the

Wild Ducks," point in this direction. Koan 53 reads: Once, when Baso and Hyakujo were walking together, they saw some wild ducks fly by. The great master asked, "What is it?" Hyakujo replied, "Wild ducks!"

"Where is it?" Master Baso asked.

Hyakujo said, "They've flown away!" Baso twisted Hyakujo's nose. Hyakujo cried out in pain.

The great master said, "When have they ever flown away?"

Zen master Bassui speaks of the second awakening in one of his letters, where he says, "The universe and yourself are of the same root, . . . you and every single thing are a unity. The gurgle of the stream and the sigh of the wind are the voices of the master. The green of pine, the white of snow, these are the colors of the master."[15] He was writing of the *sambhogakaya*.

Seeing is knowing; hearing is knowing. In essence, therefore, seeing and hearing are not different. Neither are seeing and thinking, seeing and touching, seeing and feeling. In essence, they are all one. In essence, they are all knowing.

Everything, as we have said, is the reflection of knowing. When we wake up to it, the knowing becomes obvious. Zen masters call it *mind* rather than knowing. When we do not see it, then only the trees and the birds are obvious. A turnabout, a change from the background to the foreground and the foreground to the background, must occur. The Greek-Armenian spiritual teacher G. I. Gurdjieff says, "Remember yourself," or as Dogen says, which paradoxically is the same thing, "When you forget yourself, you are one with the ten thousand things." You cannot separate the trees and the birds, the body, the walls from your knowing them, even though the ten thousand things are the ten thousand things, and knowing is knowing. All things in the six fields of senses—seeing, hearing, discernment, and knowledge—are your own awakened state. When you are in samadhi, everything that you see, hear, and touch is your own face.

It is said that everything preaches the dharma. A monk asked a master, "What is the entrance to the Way?"

The master asked, "Do you hear the sound of the stream?"

The monk said, "Yes." That is the entrance to the Way. It is not, though, if all that you hear is the sound of the stream.

The ninth ox-herding picture is concerned with the *sambhogakaya*. The verse attached to this picture says:

Returned to the origin, all is fulfilled.
It is best to be blind and deaf.[16]
He sits in his hut and does not see anything outside.[17]
The river flows and flows, just as it flows.
Red, the flower blooms just as it blooms.

Miracles do not belong to the realm of
reward and punishment.
Not-hearing is already hearing; not-seeing
already seeing.
Yesterday, in full majesty and brilliance, the sun set.
Today the dawn points.

Having passed through the furnace a thousand times,
Clearest awakening is dull compared to no-seeing,
no-hearing.
Under his straw sandals ends the way that he
once came along.
No bird sings. Red flowers bloom in glorious profusion.

## KNOWING BY DIFFERENTIATION

**Discerning principles by the light of true awareness
is the way of knowing by differentiation.**

A clear distinction must be made between discrimination and
differentiation, the third way of knowing. Yasutani once said,
"Even a cracked cup is perfect." Everything is as it is, and, as
it is, it is perfect. Someone asked Ummon, "What is Buddha?"
Ummon replied, "Dried shit." Differentiation does not imply
or bring with it any kind of judgment. In koan number 26 of
the *Mumonkan*, Zen master Hogen asks two monks to roll up
the blinds in the hall. They do so, in exactly the same way.
Hogen says, "One has it and the other does not." This is a
perfect example of differentiation, but Hogen was not discriminating one monk from the other. Zen master Mumon,
commenting on this koan, said, "Tell me, who had it and who
didn't? If your eye is single, you will see where Hogen failed.
However, I warn you strongly against discriminating has and
has not." To have a single eye is to see without discrimination. If Hogen did not discriminate, then how did he fail?
Someone said, "Everything is unique; there is no difference."
Hogen failed to see the difference.

Discrimination is dependent upon concepts and words. Just
as a net cannot capture the flowing stream, concepts and words
cannot capture the aliveness and richness of life. They dull the
bright tapestry of existence to one monotonous grey. Usefulness is a primary virtue of the discriminating mind. But judg-
ing everything according to its use also comes from the same
tendency to reduce the variety of value to one color. Someone
asked Joshu, "What is the most precious thing?"
Joshu replied, "A dead cat."

"Why is a dead cat the most precious thing?"
"Because it is useless," Joshu answered. This same tendency to one grey hue is exaggerated when even usefulness is supplanted by monetary value, the lowest common denominator of the useful. When, with awakening, this discriminating mind is "shattered," the richness and fullness of life breaks through the pale, grey cast of thought.

## THE WAY OF PERFECTION OF ACTION

**Coughing, spitting, moving the arms, activity, stillness, all that is done in harmony with the nature of reality, is called knowing through doing things. This is the sphere of freedom of the transformation body (*nirmanakaya*).**

The transformation body is the *nirmanakaya,* and this is the body that Buddha has in the world: the physical body. In terms of practice, it means yet another awakening: awakening to the fourth way of knowing. Yasutani Roshi, in the *Three Pillars of Zen,* points out, "*Ku* [*shunyata*] is not mere emptiness. It is that which is living, dynamic, devoid of mass, unfixed, beyond individuality or personality—the matrix of all phenomena"[18] The universe is not static; it is dynamic, alive. Action is the way of life: even the flowers reach up to the sun and the trees spread out their arms. Someone asked Zen master Joshu, "What is my essence?" Joshu said, "The tree sways, the bird flies about, the fish leaps, the water is muddy."

A master will ask, "Who walks? Who talks?" Sometimes a hapless student will claim, "I do." But what muscles will he use, what nerves? We can exercise self-will as much as we like, but still the body does not rise. How fascinating it is that we

talk and yet do not know the words we are going to use until
we have said them. When I walk, the universe walks; and my
dancing and songs are, as Hakuin tells us, the voice of the
dharma.

Knowing-in-action is sometimes called the "function." A
*mondo* (question and answer) helps make the point more clear.

A master and his student were hoeing a field. The monk
asked, "What is it?"

The master stood up and planted his hoe in the ground.

The monk said, "You have the essence, you do not have the
function."

The master said, "Then what is it?"

The monk went on hoeing.

The master said, "You have the function, you do not have
the essence."

Zen master Yuishun makes a similar point when, coming to
awakening, he wrote:

> Why, it's but the motion of eyes and brows!
> And here I've been seeking it far and wide.
> Awakened at last, I find the moon
> Above the pines, the river surging high.[19]

Everything that we do is the dharma in action; everything
that we do is the samadhi of action. When we ask, "Who
walks?" we inquire about the samadhi of action. The samadhi
of walking walks; the samadhi of seeing sees; the samadhi of
talking talks. Samadhi is all. Let me repeat, this is the samadhi
that cannot be attained, the samadhi that is your true nature.
It is your state right now. Your state is a state of samadhi. It is
just mind only.

The tenth ox-herding picture tells of the *nirmanakaya*:

With bare chest and feet he enters the market.
His face is smothered with dirt, his head covered
  with ashes.
A huge laugh breaks out on his face.
Not lowering himself to perform miracles
Or wonders, he suddenly makes the withered
  trees bloom.
In a friendly manner this fellow comes from
  a foreign race.[20]
Now he is Peter, now he is Paul.
When, like a flash of lightning, he wields
  the iron staff.[21]
Wide open spring the doors and gates.

Like a bolt from the blue, the iron staff springs.
Sometimes he speaks Hunnish, sometimes Chinese,
  laughing out loud.
Understand how to meet yourself, but remain
  unknown to the self—
The palace gate will open wide.

At this level, perfect interpenetration abides. Neither awakening nor illusion lingers; oneness and twoness are no more.

## THE IMPORTANCE OF CONTINUING PRACTICE AFTER AWAKENING

Hakuin is saying that awakening has different aspects, each of which can be gradually deepened. These are different aspects of our fundamental intelligence or fundamental wisdom. Awakening is the conception, you might say, of the Buddha-seed. This Buddha-seed can also be called the *bodhichitta,* the mind that seeks the way. It is the true beginning of the possibility each of us has of being human in the fullest sense.

**Even so, you still do not see the way with complete clarity, and your power of shining insight is not yet fully mature. Therefore, if you do not go on with your practice, you will be like a merchant who hoards his capital and doesn't engage in trade. In this way, not only does he never become rich, but eventually he even goes broke through spending just to keep up the appearance of being wealthy.**

The fourth patriarch told a monk, Gozu, who was deeply awakened, "You should not contemplate, nor should you purify your mind. . . . Be boundless and absolutely free from all conditions." In other words, the patriarch was saying that it was not necessary to undertake any definite, further discipline. We must remember, though, that the fourth patriarch was a teacher in China during the Tang dynasty and therefore was talking at a time when the dharma was flourishing. Furthermore, Gozu's awakening was very deep and thoroughgoing.

By Hakuin's time, the dharma had deteriorated considerably; and in our time, the dharma has deteriorated even more. Many people wonder, "When I have seen through my koan, when I have seen into my true nature, what else will there be to do?" Hakuin is pointing out that kensho, even though it may seem to be a deep awakening, is still only a beginning.

**What do I mean by going on with your practice? It is like a merchant engaged in trade who spends a hundred dollars to make a profit of a thousand. In this way he**

accumulates vast wealth and treasure, and so becomes free to do as he will with his blessings. Whether rich or poor, money is still money, but without engaging in trade, it is impossible to get rich. Even if your breakthrough to reality is genuine, if your power of shining insight is weak, you cannot break down the barriers of habitual actions. Unless your knowing of differentiation is clear, you cannot benefit sentient beings according to their abilities. Therefore, you must know the essential road of gradual practice.

Most people do not understand this. They say, "I thought this guy was awakened, and look at him, look at the way he is acting, look at the way he is talking, look at the way he is reacting. What good is awakening if this is all that it amounts to? I thought he was going to be perfect." One gets this kind of reaction mostly from people who are playing with practice, or not practicing at all. People who are really practicing, who know the bitterness of the struggle, have nothing but sympathy for those who fail and fall on the path. They have the urge to reach forward and help them back on their feet again. The way is hard and difficult, and a kensho, even if it is a deep kensho, still doesn't make that way any easier. Each step of the way has to be walked—and sometimes it is like walking over sharp cobblestones in bare feet. One has to go on, though; one has gone too far to go back.

What are the habitual actions that Hakuin is talking about? We are thrown into the world and are quite confused by it. Our first years are like trying to stand up, without supports, in the face of a strong wind. We are constantly blown over. Therefore, we do whatever we can to survive in the moment, regardless of the long-term cost. During World War II, a fighter plane called the Spitfire was used in action. Its throttle could be pushed through a gate and the engine given a special boost. The pilot could use this in case of an emergency to get away from an enemy aircraft. A cost, of course, was attached to the use of this booster. The frame of the plane could be shaken to pieces.

When we are young, we live a good part of our time with the throttle through the gate. With this in mind, one begins to understand what great force we use to establish the habitual reactions that we are talking about. One also begins to appreciate the energy we put into maintaining them. Sometimes when we are young we have nightmares, and the whole world opens up as a vortex about to swallow us, engulf us completely. This is no kid stuff we are talking about now; it seems that we have to use every particle of our being to continue to be. We have to stand up to face our parents—they are six-foot giants and we are two feet and a bit—and we have to somehow win this contest or nothing, it seems, will be left of us; we will be eaten up entirely. Our barriers are like smelted iron, tempered steel. Therefore, when later we try to melt them down, the task is by no means an easy one. We should not be surprised that, as Dogen said, it takes sweat, tears, and sometimes blood to make them malleable again.

Zen master Issan said that even though, through practice, the original mind has been awakened so that one is instantaneously awakened to knowing, the inertia of habit still lingers.[22] This habit has been formed since the beginning of time, and cannot be completely banished in one go. One must therefore be taught to cut off completely the stream of one's habitual ideas and views that are held in place by unresolved karma. This process of purification is practice.

Yasutani Roshi used to say the following: Suppose you are

in a completely dark cave. If you then light a match, the "quality" of the cave will change completely. It will now be filled with light, and no longer be completely dark. If you then light a candle from the match, the intensity of the light will increase, but this is a quantitative change, not a qualitative one. If, with the help of the candle, you find a flashlight and turn it on, the intensity will increase again. One could go on increasing the intensity until eventually one might break though the roof of the cave and let the sunlight flood in. Although the intensity of the light is different in each case, qualitatively sunlight is no different from the light of the match.

Hakuin says that this subsequent practice is essential if one wishes to fulfill the potential offered by the first awakening. Indeed it could be said that a first awakening, even if it is deep, very rarely has the power to transform a person. The value of the first awakening is that it enables us to arouse great faith, so much so that efforts that previously were arduous to sustain become less arduous. We can compare it to clearing up the basement. If the basement is completely dark, then it will be very difficult to clear it up. Indeed, one could make the mess a great deal worse. If one has even just a faint light, the work becomes considerably easier. Even so, the basement still needs to be cleaned up.

### What is Great Perfect Mirror knowing?

Zen masters frequently use the metaphor of the mirror.[23] A famous example is the interchange involving Hui-neng (Jap.: Eno). The fifth patriarch wanted to pass on the patriarchate. In order to determine who should be chosen, he asked his monks to write a short poem to indicate their level of attainment. The head monk wrote:

The body is a Bodhi tree,
The mind a mirror bright.
Wipe it carefully day by day
And let no dust alight.

Hui-neng realized that the head monk had not seen into his true nature, and he wrote instead:

In Bodhi there is no tree,
Nor a mirror bright,
From the beginning not a thing is,
Where can the dust alight?

In this interchange, Hui-neng insists on no mirror. This dispute between the head monk and Hui-neng probably had its origins in the struggle that was going on at this time between Taoism and Buddhism. The verse of the head monk is suspiciously like a quote from the Taoist master Chuang-tzu, "When a mirror is clear, it is because it has not the least amount of dust on it. If there is any dust, the mirror is not clear."[24] The aim of the Taoist is to have a perfectly still mind. As Chuang-tzu also says, "It is not in running water that men mirror themselves but in stilled water." This stillness is an underlying substratum of some kind. The fourth Zen patriarch writes, "I say that Chuang-tzu still had a mind obstructed by the notion of One. Lao-tzu says that in the profound mystery lies a subtle spirit. This is because he keeps to the idea of an inner mind, even though he has let go of an outside. . . . Lao-tzu stagnates in the mind and in consciousness."[25]

Tetougen comments further on this debate in China over attachment to the still mind by quoting a former master who said: "It is by maintaining tranquility that the Confucianists of the Sung dynasty became attached to the state of mind which did not allow any feeling of joy, anger, sadness or pleasure to arise. It is just by maintaining tranquility that Lao-tzu insists that one finally arrives at nothing and so comes to tranquility and serenity."[26]

In Zen, the metaphor of a mirror is used to point out that, just as reflections do not have any being in themselves and are dependent upon the mirror for their being, our experiences have no being in themselves and are dependent upon knowing for their being. This is like saying that form is emptiness. Zen insists upon no substratum, no underlying or Supreme Being. The doctrine of *prajna,* an aroused mind that abides nowhere, affirms this, as does Buddha's doctrine of *anicca,* the doctrine of no-thingness. For Zen, the mirror is knowing, which, although it is not constant, nevertheless constantly and at each instant recreates itself. Knowing is its own being; being is itself knowing. For the Taoist, the mirror is the substratum that makes reflections possible, hence the need for a clean and tranquil mirror. Hui-neng put his fist through this substratum.

**if you want to see into this great matter, you must first generate great will, great faith, and great determination to see through the originally inherent, awakened nature.**

Hakuin is saying that deep, deep questioning must pervade our lives. "What is it?" Everything must point to this question: "What is this?" We use words and expressions such as *knowing, intelligence, supreme wisdom, mirror wisdom, bodhisattvas,* or *Buddha-nature.* We wonder what the words mean and so use other words as definitions, and then wonder in turn what those words mean. What use are all these jangling words? And *what is asking the question?* That which asks the question and that which is asked about, are they different? We cannot step outside of this enigma for a moment. What is it? It holds and supports us, it was with us at conception, it will be with us at death, it will be with us in whatever *bardo* realms may exist. It is never absent; when we sleep, when we laugh, when we talk, when we walk—it is talking, it is walking, it is laughing, it is sleeping, it is dying. We are it. What is it?

At the Montreal Zen Center, before a member is accepted as a student, he or she must answer three questions. First, do I really want to see into my true nature, or am I simply "practicing Zen," wanting to find peace and comfort or whatever? Second, am I prepared to do the work that is necessary, and to go on doing it until I have penetrated to the root? Finally, do I have faith in the teacher, and will I be prepared to give him the benefit of the doubt when necessary? If the student can answer "yes" to all three, then he or she is accepted as a student. In this way, a commitment is made; it is a commitment not to the Zen center, not to Zen, nor to the teacher— but to oneself. A true commitment can only be made if one can generate the great faith, the great doubt, and the great perseverance necessary to sustain the practice of Zen.

**After great will, faith, and determination are aroused, you should then constantly ask, "Who is the host of seeing and hearing?" Walking, standing, sitting, lying down, active or silent, whether in favorable or unfavorable circumstances, throw your mind into the question of what it is that sees everything here and now. What hears?**

The koan "Who am I?" which is sometime asked as "What am I?" underlies these questions. It is a question asked by Japanese and Chinese Zen Buddhists, by Tibetan Buddhists, by Sufis, and by Hindus. Quite recently the late Pope Jean Paul II said Christians too must ponder this question. Two Hindu teachers, Ramana Maharshi and Nisargadatta Maharaj, have made the question more popular in recent years. Ramana Maharshi says:

> The mind will subside only by means of the inquiry, "Who am I?" The thought "Who am I?", destroying all other thoughts, will itself finally be destroyed like the stick used for stirring the funeral pyre. If other thoughts rise one should, without attempting to complete them, inquire, "To whom did they rise?" What does it matter however many thoughts rise? At the very moment that each thought rises, if one vigilantly inquires "To whom did this rise?", it will be known "to me." If one then inquires "Who am I?", the mind will turn back to its source [the Self] and the thought which had risen will also subside. By repeatedly practicing thus, the power of the mind to abide in its source increases.[27]

And Nisargadatta says, "Give up all questions except one: 'Who am I?' After all, the only fact that you are sure of is that you are. The 'I am' is certain. The 'I am this' is not. Struggle to find out what you are in reality."[28]

In Japanese, the koan is asked in this way: "What is your face before your parents were born?" I sometimes ask, "Before the question 'who am I?' arises, what are you?"

Question like this, ponder like this—ultimately, what
is it? If you keep on doubting continuously, with a bold
spirit and a feeling of shame urging you on, your effort
will naturally become unified and solid, turning into
a single mass of doubt throughout heaven and earth.
The spirit will feel suffocated, the mind distressed,
like a bird in a cage, like a rat that has gone into
a bamboo tube and cannot escape.

Please note the word *ponder*, from the Latin word *ponderare*
meaning "to weigh." It implies a profound way of thinking, a
profound use of the mind. The question "Who am I?" is not
just a blind push in the dark, it is not simply battering our
heads; it is using our mind, pondering. The word *ponder* has
a certain sense of weight, or gravity, about it. At this level of
thought, words no longer help us, but we can still think. It is
what Dogen called "thinking the unthinkable." Someone
asked him, "How does one think the unthinkable?" He replied,
"Without thought." That is, without concepts, ideas, words,
and thoughts. But one thinks. It is entirely possible to do this.
Many people, when they practice with a koan, reach the limit
of words, then the limit of conceptual thinking, then they reach
the limit of intuition, and then they give up. "What is the use?"
they ask. "It is impossible." In Zen, the journey only begins
when all roads end. We do not have to be a super-person. People who do break through the gateless gate are people like you
and me. To put the work aside and say, "This kind of practice
is alright for Buddha or Hakuin or whatever, these guys had
time, they didn't have families and all that distraction. I had
better wait until next time round." No. This is our work, and
it is our work now. Now, at this moment, as we sit here at
home, or work, or in a meditation room. What is it that hears?

What is it that resists this question at this moment? Questioning like this, pondering like this, what is it?

## a feeling of shame urging you on

A feeling of shame! It is not that we are ashamed because we can't resolve the question. If we really work at this question, eventually a sense of shame, of remorse, even a sense of unworthiness comes up. This recalls Nicodemus in the New Testament saying, "Lord, I am not worthy," or Buddha's calling upon the earth to bear witness to his worthiness. When it arises, we work with shame, with unworthiness. "Repent and be saved." Repentance arises when everything begins to return home, when everything comes together. The turnabout has already begun when repentance appears. Everything is becoming one. This is why humiliation is such an important aspect of work. Humiliation teaches us humility, and humility teaches us remorse.

The French spiritual philosopher and psychologist Hubert Benoit, in his book *The Supreme Doctrine,* said this about humiliation:

> The whole problem of human suffering is summed up in the problem of humiliation. To be free of suffering is to be free from the possibility of being humiliated. Where does humiliation come from? From seeing myself powerless? No, that is not enough. It comes from the fact that I try in vain not to see my real powerlessness. It is not powerlessness itself that causes humiliation, but the shock experienced by my claim to be unique, when it comes up against the reality of things. I am not humiliated because the world

denied me, but because I was unable to overcome this denial. The cause of my suffering never lies in the outside world; it is the result of the claim that I put out and which is broken against the wall of reality. I deceive myself when I say that the world has thrown itself against me and hurt me; it is I who have hurt myself. When I no longer claim uniqueness, nothing will ever hurt me again.

If a humiliating experience turns up, offering me a marvelous opportunity to see into myself, at once the imagination throws up some supposed danger. In short, I constantly defend myself against that which offers to save me; I fight inch by inch to protect the very source of my unhappiness.

I will stop fighting against the constructive and harmonizing benefits of humiliation to the degree to which I can understand that my true well-being is to be found, paradoxically, where, until now, I have thought that my pain resided.

I will see that all my negative states are, at bottom, humiliations. I will then be able to feel myself humiliated, annoyed, without any image arising in me other than this state, and will be able to remain there motionless, my understanding having got rid of the reflex attempts at flight. From the moment that I succeed in no longer moving in my humiliated state, I discover to my surprise that there is an "asylum of rest," the unique harbor of safety, the only place in the world in which I can find complete security. I feel myself nearer to the ground, nearer to real humility, humility that is not the acceptance of my inferiority, but the abandonment of my claim to be unique.[29]

People often say to me, "You always talk about suffering." One of the members of the Montreal Zen Center went to see another teacher not so long ago and, when he came back, told me that this teacher had said to him, "Enjoy your zazen." He then asked me, "Why don't you say things like that?" I could only reply that it is because we have to pass through this dark night of the soul, and that passing through this dark night of the soul is our fulfillment, is our totality; in this is our true "enjoyment." We are not talking in terms of misery that we cannot support. We are talking about the suffering that is necessary for birth, for rebirth.

I do not mean that we have to actively seek humiliation. The world is ready to hit you with its club as you walk through the door, so don't worry, be patient, it will in time do its work for you.

A clear distinction must be made between shame and being ashamed. One is ashamed in the presence of others. Shame is a personal and private feeling. It arises when two separate and incongruous impulses occur in our presence. When two conflicting impulses arise, a tension also arises. For example, I want to be an honest man and I want to be a rich man. I then come to have the possibility to steal a large sum of money. As I contemplate these two alternatives, being honest and being rich, with money in easy reach, a feeling of guilt will arise. The guilt comes from a tension and from the attempt to restore unity, harmony. We can resist and try to overcome the feeling of guilt by having one or other of the impulses triumph. If I succumb and steal the money, then I will have to bury the feeling of wanting to be an honest man, or transform the situation in my mind so that my actions are no longer stealing but "getting what is due to me," or something similar. This will simply translate the guilt into profound insecurity, the original conflict constantly threatening to break though. If we stay with the pain of shame or guilt, on the other hand, then gradually underlying unity will prevail.

We are divided against ourselves in the very core of our being. This division is the ultimate source of shame and guilt; it is, moreover, what makes humiliation possible. Ignorance is to ignore, or turn our back on, our true nature. But, as I have said, ignoring our true nature does not make it disappear. Our true nature is One, whole, holy, but when we turn our back on our true nature, we are two in our manifestation. We are wounded in our being.

The story of Adam and Eve tells the same story, although more concretely. They turned their back on God. They chose the tree of good and bad, the tree of dualism. This is the original sin and the ultimate source of guilt and shame. Guilt and shame tend to pervade the lives of many people who have not been able to create adequate buffers to shield themselves from these feelings. Hakuin is urging us to let the feeling of shame and guilt surge up in ourselves. By doing this, we allow the basic unity, which is our true nature, to break through and become the foundation of our lives.[30]

In the confessional one must repent, one must also feel the shame and the guilt. In the confessional we are given penances, payments that we have to make for our sins. But the shame is already the payment; it is already the absolution. But it must be sincere shame, sincere remorse.

**The spirit will feel suffocated, the mind distressed, like a bird in a cage, like a rat that has gone into a bamboo tube and cannot escape.**

At this stage you are no longer working on the question "Who am I?" The question is now working on you. You don't know where you are, who you are, why you are. It is as if you surf on the waves of the ocean and are caught on the wrong side of a wave. It throws you; all you can do is go with it. You just go; you just carry on. You might feel panic, the fear of being out of control. But, we must go back again, back again, and back again to the question.

The image of a rat in a bamboo tube is a favorite metaphor for Hakuin. He sometimes adds that the rat cannot go forward and cannot retreat, but cannot stay where it is. It is the ultimate double bind. Yasutani Roshi used to say something similar: that it is like swallowing a hot rice cake—one cannot swallow it and one cannot cough it up, but it is too uncomfortable to just leave it. Koans ultimately push us to this state. A master says, "If you call this a stick, I will give you thirty blows. If you say it is not a stick, I will give you thirty blows. What is it?" The social scientist Gregory Bateson, who introduced the expression "double bind," used this koan to illustrate what he meant by the term.

**At this time, if you just keep going without falling back, you will feel that you are entering a crystal world; the whole world, inside and outside, mats and ceiling, houses and cars, fields and mountains, grasses and trees, people and animals, utensils and goods, all are as they are but like illusions, like dreams, like shadows, like smoke. When you open your eyes clearly with presence of mind and see with certainty, an inconceivable realm appears that seems to exist, yet also seems not to exist in a way. This is called the time when the knowing essence becomes manifest.**

As you go on, it becomes increasingly a joint effort—you and
the universe begin working together. All the suffering that
previously held you back, all the obstacles and obstructions,
now become grist for the mill. A time comes when it is just
as though you go over a hill and you can make tremendous
effort without any effort at all. This is the time of the "ten-
foot Buddha."

**all are as they are but like illusions, like dreams,
like shadows, like smoke.**

The universe is totally unobstructed at that moment. You feel
you can walk through walls. The whole world is suspended in
a kind of translucent way.

**When you open your eyes clearly with presence of mind
and see with certainty, an inconceivable realm appears
that seems to exist, yet also seems not to exist in a way.**

It is an inconceivable realm because we no longer have any
thought about it. It's a world of clarity, of purity. However, we
don't think "how clear, how pure." It is a realm where "I know"
is no longer simply the background. It permeates all. It is like
a scrim. When the light is in front of the scrim it lights up the
pattern on the scrim. The pattern is obvious. But when the light
is behind the scrim, the pattern is hazy and the light is all.

The poet A. E. Housman said that he was "a stranger and
afraid in a world I never made." But, on the contrary, by knowing the world, I make it *my world*. This computer is "my" computer, these books are "interesting," and that tax form is a
"nuisance." Of course, my world is not just a world of facts, it
is also a world of facts inextricably mixed with a world of val-

ues and meanings, a world intrinsically colored by my prefer-
ences, by my hopes, fears, longings, lusts, and doubts. When
the light shines on the scrim of life, I know these facts, values,
and meanings—they are all too obvious. When that same light
is behind the scrim, when knowing is no longer overlooked,
then all that was plain and obvious becomes like a dream. The
Zen masters tirelessly assure us that "it is right before your
nose!" "It is under your feet." "It's like one in water crying 'I
thirst!'"

Gurdjieff said, "Man does not remember himself." Human
beings forget their own half of the equation. It is said, "When
thoughts of the dharma are weak, thoughts of the world are
strong; when thoughts of the dharma are strong, thoughts of
the world are weak."

**This is called the time when the knowing essence
becomes manifest.**

The light is behind the scrim; the essence of experience is
knowing. Knowing is the essence of all, the essence of everything that exists.

To change the metaphor: it is like seeing a film. All that we
see at a film is but the modifications of the white light. Nevertheless, throughout the film, we ignore the white light. Even
so, the white light is the essence of all that is seen.

## THE GATE OF INSPIRATION

**If you think this is wonderful and extraordinary and
joyfully become infatuated and attached to this, you
will, after all, fall into the cave of demons and will never
see the real, awakened nature.**

So often, we get a deep insight, an insight that can be profound enough to change the very way that we understand the world, and we then feel that we have arrived, fully awakened. The way that we normally understand the world is founded on such tenuous foundations that a deep insight can completely overturn it and bring a drastically new comprehension of everything. No wonder there are so many self-styled gurus in the world, so many new answers to old questions.

Bassui, in his letters, warns us of this stage. He says:

> [Some people think] that in the practice of Zen a decisive point has been reached when one feels a deep void with awareness of neither inner nor outer, the entire body having become shining, transparent, and clear like a blue sky on a bright day.
>
> This last appears when the true nature begins to manifest itself, but it cannot be called genuine Self-realization. Zen masters of old would call it the "deep pit of pseudo-emancipation." Those who reach this stage, believing they have no more problems in [the study and practice of] Buddhism, behave haughtily through lack of wisdom and engage eagerly in debates on religion, taking delight in cornering their opponents but becoming angry when cornered themselves.[31]

When I awaken to the truth that my world is founded upon knowing, that it is dependent on knowing, a revolution occurs. But the story does not end here. This is why Hakuin goes on to say:

**At this point, if you do not fondly cling to your state but arouse your spirit to wholehearted effort, from time to time you will experience such things as forgetting you are sitting when you are sitting, forgetting about standing when you are standing, forgetting your own body, forgetting the world around you.**

This is samadhi. Anyone who has attended a Zen *sesshin* or retreat will know these moments when it seems that time stops. Afterward, one does not know whether one slept or was awake. But these timeless moments reveal a reality more intense than any experienced by our ordinary consciousness. The sense "I am doing this" falls away, and with it goes the gap, the void, the wound that haunts the heart of being.

Still one must go on.

**Then, if you keep going without retreating, the conscious spirit will suddenly shatter and the awakened nature will appear all at once.**

One of the hallmarks of genuine awakening is that it is sudden and unexpected.

The following *satori* poem by Zen master Muso Kokushi says it well:

Vainly I dug for a perfect sky,
Piling a barrier all around.
Then one black night, lifting a heavy
Tile, I crushed the skeletal void![32]

As we said above, the shattering of the discriminating mind does not mean that it breaks into pieces, it is already in pieces;

shattering means that it is discovered to be One whole. Our true nature is One. Like everything else that is fundamental, we take this Oneness for granted. We overlook it. Though it shows itself as interest, desire, intention, and attention, and though it sustains the world at the micro- and macroscopic levels—though it heals our wounds and makes the sick well; though we create, walk, dance, skate, run, and jump by it; and though civilization and culture would be impossible without it—we take it for granted and overlook it.

We overlook it because the discriminating mind breaks up the whole in the same way that a shattered mirror distorts reality. Each facet of the mirror reflects its own whole. From this perspective, the perspective of consciousness, multiplicity is too immediate for Oneness to have any real power. However, when this shattering is itself shattered, Oneness shines through; it can only shine through as One, it cannot come in parts, gradually.

**This is the Great Perfect Mirror knowing.**[33]

The Great Perfect Mirror *is* knowing. You look around the room and see the room. You do not see the seeing, the knowing. After you come to awakening, knowing is all. In the words of the Hindu song, "The Lord is in my eye. That is why I see him everywhere."

This is why it is said that the world is a dream. A dream is an experience in which the knowing is as important as what is known. Dreaming, we dream that the dream is real, and ignore the knowing.

The Great Perfect Mirror way of knowing is kensho. It could also be called the complete perfect awakening. One master, on coming to kensho, said:

The moon is still the same old moon
The flowers are not different,
Now I see that I am the thingness
Of all the things I see.

And Buddha said, "Throughout heaven and earth, I alone am the honored one." Another master, on his awakening, said, "Oh!"

Hakuin says:

**This is the first stage of inspiration; you can discern the source of eighty thousand doctrines, with their limitless subtle meanings, all at once. As one becomes, all become; as one decays, all decay—nothing is lacking, no principle is not complete.**

All the Tripitaka, the collection of Buddhist scriptures, all the koans and *mondo,* have their origin here. To see through a speck of dust is to see through the whole universe. The salt in a drop of the sea is no different from all the salt in the whole ocean. During World War II, when I was young in England, I sometimes helped farmers to reap, stack, and thrash their corn. These were the days before the combine harvester. The harvest would be then kept in sacks in the barn. An agent would later come around to buy the produce. He would not need to examine the contents of all the sacks. It would be enough to take one handful from one sack and let it run through his fingers.

**As a newborn child of Buddha, the new bodhisattva will reveal the sun of wisdom of the awakened nature; but even so, the clouds of his former actions will not have yet been cleared away.**

This is remarkably similar to what Chinul, the great twelfth-century Korean Zen master said:

> Although he has awakened to the fact that his original nature is no different from that of the Buddhas, the beginningless habit-energies are extremely difficult to remove suddenly, and so he must continue to cultivate while relying on this awakening. Through this gradual permeation, his endeavors reach completion. He constantly nurtures the sacred embryo, and after a long time he becomes a saint. Hence it is called gradual cultivation. This process can be compared to the maturation of a child. From the day of its birth, a baby is endowed with all the sense organs just like everyone else, but its strength is not yet fully developed. It is only after many months and years that it will finally become an adult.[34]

Our problem is that we say, "I am this." "I am" is the truth; "I am this, not that" is the problem. A nun said, "I cannot pull up the weed because if I do so, I shall pull up the flower." The flower is "I am"; the weed is "this, not that." With kensho we let go of the weed, the "thingness" of the thing. To say "'I am' is the truth" is not quite right. It might be better to say that "'I am' is the *doorway* to the truth." Originally we are Buddha, One. Yet, through ignorance, we are divided against ourselves. Because we are One, but two, we suffer. The Sanskrit word for suffering is *duhkha*, which is related to duality, or twoness. Through suffering unity reasserts itself, but "downstream" of the initial separation. Although unity is still unity, it is now colored by duality. The original purity is covered by *I–It,* that is "I–the world," "I–him (or her)," or "I–the emotions." "I" is the emissary of the original purity; it is the flower. The weed is what *I* is identified with: the world, him or her, the emotions, and all the myriad other identifications. Most of us are identified with our bodies, some are identified with their possessions, others with their jobs, others with their image, and others yet are identified with their suffering. As a rule, the word *I* is first used by a child at about the age of two, the age that many parents know as the *terrible twos.* At this age the child not only uses the word *I*, but he or she also uses the word *no.* I saw an example of the terrible twos after my grandson had his second birthday. Every now and again he would say "NO," and the very heavens heard him say it. We took him for a walk once when we were visiting my son, a fighter pilot who was living with his family in Germany. The little boy decided to take his cart along with him. After a while, for some reason or other, he decided he had had enough of the cart, and so put it down and walked away. Well, we couldn't leave the cart there, so I suggested to him that he pick it up.

"No."

I said, "You will lose it if you leave it there. Pick it up."

"No!" I went back to pick it up myself. He looked at me, pointing and shaking a tiny, peremptory finger at me as he cried "NO!!" All the neighbors came out, heads popped out of windows, doors whipped open—what was this? My grandson was establishing something stable in a terribly unstable world. He had to pin this world down, and he pinned it down with this tremendous assertion. With flushed face, the veins in his forehead and neck like cords, glaring eyes, and trembling finger, he said "NO!" Just imagine yourself putting everything into making a statement like that, and doing it several times a day.

We create a barrier around ourselves with this "NO!" We do so, most often, when we feel threatened, and react with fear, anger, rage, and hatred. This is why the barrier is cast in steel—steel that is constantly tempered by our constant conflicts and wars with the world, others, and ourselves. We may come to awakening, but the steel around us remains strong. It can only be melted down and dissolved after having been repeatedly passed through the furnace. This is why a simple awakening is not enough. Ramana Maharshi spent six long, arduous years melting down his own barriers after his initial awakening at the age of seventeen, and he was a very gentle soul to begin with.

I learned something about barriers after World War II, when I was employed while a student to break up the air-raid shelters that we had used as protection against the German bombs. During the war these shelters were most precious; after the war they were no longer necessary. But breaking up the shelters was very hard work.

Because one's power in the way is weak and one's perception of reality is not perfectly clear, the Great Perfect Mirror wisdom is associated with the easterly direction and called the Gate of Inspiration. It is like the sun rising in the east—although the mountains, rivers, and land receive the sun's rays, they are not yet warmed by its light. Although you may have seen the way clearly, if your power of shining through is not strong enough, you may be blocked by inherent and chronic afflictions, and will still not be free and independent in both agreeable and adverse situations. This is like someone who has been looking for an ox and who may one day see through to the real ox, but if he doesn't hold the halter firmly to hold it in check, it will, sooner or later, run away.

We have already encountered the ox as a way of talking about true nature. The ox would have been as familiar to the seventeenth-century Japanese peasant as the car is to us today. It was a beast of burden, and the peasant relied upon it as we rely upon the internal combustion engine.

In the first of the ten ox-herding pictures, a boy is shown running around looking for his ox. Who is it that is lost? Is it the boy, or the ox? A story is told of an American explorer who was out hunting with an Inuit hunter. While they were tracking their prey, a snowstorm broke out and they had to run for shelter. After the storm was spent, they emerged from the shelter, and the American looked around in dismay to find the landscape had completely changed. All the old landmarks had been wiped away. The American turned in despair and said to the hunter, "We are lost." The hunter replied, "We not lost; igloo lost."

Anyone who has searched for a spiritual way knows the feeling of desolation and hopelessness that can overtake us when we feel that our true home is lost. We feel a desperation bordering upon panic. We reach the stage where we do not know where to look, why to look, or what to look for, and yet, somehow, look we must.

The second picture in the ox-herding series shows the little boy following the tracks of the ox. This is like when we have found a way and a teacher. We listen to what he or she says, and we hear, every now and then, the ring of truth. Something real is calling. We have seen the tracks of the ox. One's lassitude and despair give way to a new kind of energy, a delight. The ox is real, but still it cannot be found. To find it, all that is required is the will to continue. As the verse says:

By the withered tree in front of the cliff.
Many wrong turnings

Lead him astray
Caught, like a bird in a nest covered with grass
Round and around he turns in the small cave.
Does he know he's gone astray?
Just at the moment when his feet, in searching, follow
    the traces
He misses the ox and lets him escape.

But then, one day the boy sees the ox:

Suddenly, the bush warbler's clear voice sings from
    the treetops.
A warm sun, a gentle breeze, green willows by the river.
No longer can the ox hide
How magnificent the head with its soaring horns
How can it be depicted?

Head-on the herdsman crashes into the ox.
No longer does he need to pursue the bellowing.
This ox is neither blue nor white.
The herdsman nods to himself, smiling quietly.
Neither brush nor crayon could depict the wonderful
    landscape.

This moment has been described as "a tree without roots, a
land where there is neither light nor shade, a mountain valley
where a shout does not echo."

**Once you have seen the ox, make ox herding your only
concern. Without this practice, after awakening, many
people who have seen reality miss the boat. Therefore, to
reach knowing of equality, do not linger in Great Perfect**

**Mirror knowing. Go on and on, concentrate on practice after awakening.**

Let me repeat, to see is to see all. See through one speck of dust, see through the whole universe. Nevertheless, as Hakuin says, to bring fully into awareness what you have seen, this later work is necessary. You have moved out of your mindsets, the structures of the mind and your worldview. You have made the leap from the jug to the clay. Nevertheless, you must not dwell there or you will not be able to move around in this awakening. Koan number 25 of the *Hekigan-roku* says:

> The hermit of the Lotus Flower Peak held up his staff and said to the assembly: "When the ancients got here, why did they not agree to stay?"
>
> Receiving no answer, he answered for them, "Because it is of no use on the path of life." Again he asked, "After all, what will you do with it?" He gave a verse that said,
>
> > With my staff across my shoulder
> > I pay no attention to others
> > I go straight into the numberless peaks.

## THE GATE OF PRACTICE

**First, with the intimate perception, which you have had into knowing itself, enlighten all worlds with radiant insight.**

This is going into the myriad peaks. Climbing to the peak of a mountain is an analogy for coming to awakening. One goes up the mountain for oneself, but down the mountain for others. The hermit is saying, never mind about one awakening, there are numberless peaks, do not stay sitting on top of one. Another master said, "Peak upon peak of snow covered mountains." No matter how weak or shallow our initial awakening might be, we nevertheless work with it. In the book *To Know Yourself,* I used the analogy of someone trying to light a fire using damp leaves and having only one match.[35] You take the match and light just a few leaves. You nurse the fire and then you add a few more leaves, nurse the flame again, and then add a few twigs. Then you add a few bigger twigs, then some bigger twigs still. In this way, you build the fire until you can add a small branch, then a couple of small branches. Now you start adding some logs, and before you know it, you have the whole forest afire. But if you begin by trying to burn the forest, you just put out the little match. We must always start from where we are; this is as true after awakening as before. We must not impose upon ourselves images or ideas of how we ought to be.

You start where you are. You take your question as it is. If it is a feeble question, then work with it as a feeble question; nurse it, nurture it. It's like coaxing a small flame on which you blow gently. A gale will just blow it out. If you stay close to it, if you don't move away from it for a moment, if you tend it carefully, it will grow into a more meaningful question. Now you can start putting some pressure on it, you can start leaning on it a little. Then it gets to be an intense question and you can start pushing right into it. So it goes. All the time the question burns from within; it is not imposed from without.

**When you see something, shine through it; when you hear, shine through what you are hearing; shine through the five *skandhas*; shine though the six fields of sense**

perception—in front, behind, left and right, through seven calamities and eight disasters, become one with radiant vision of the whole body. See through all things, internal and external; shine through them. When this work becomes solid, then perception of reality will be perfectly, distinctly clear, just like looking at the palm of you hand.

At this point, while increasing the use of this clear knowing and insight, if you enter awakening, then shine though awakening. If you get into agreeable circumstances, then shine through agreeable circumstances. If you fall into adverse situations, then shine through adverse situations. When greed or desire arise, shine though greed and desire; when hatred or anger arise, shine through hatred and anger; when you act out of ignorance, shine through ignorance. When the three poisons of hatred, greed, and ignorance are no more, and the mind is pure, shine through that pure mind. At all times, in all places, be it desires, senses, gain, loss, right, wrong, visions of Buddha or of dharma, in all things shine through with your whole body.

When you go to a movie, if it is a good film, you are completely taken in by it, absorbed by it; you are one with it in a somnolent, unaware way. You become identified with the characters—you love the hero and heroine and hate the villain. When the hero marries the heroine you are happy, and when the hero gets hurt you are sad. The plot goes backward and forward and you are quite taken up with it; you are right in there, part of it. This is the art of the storyteller, to draw you into her story.

Now supposing somebody were to take a flashlight and shine

it on the back of the screen. This used to happen when I was young and would go to see Charlie Chaplin films in the church hall. The screen was often just somebody's sheet hung up there on a frame in the middle of the hall. I would be completely involved with Charlie, then, all of a sudden, someone would hunt around for something behind the screen with a flashlight. That ruined the film. I could no longer be taken in by it. What was once real and opaque, when the light shines through, is shown to be transparent and illusory.

Hakuin is saying that after awakening, something similar to this is necessary. One defuses, reduces the power, reduces the force of the situation by shining through it. One does this by seeing that everything is one seamless whole. Instead of looking for unity within phenomena, one sees phenomena as unity. The whole push and shove of life, the ambition for unity, and the striving to be the unique, outstanding one, is reduced. It doesn't just drop away like a dead limb overnight, it takes a long time to be free of this; but you are defusing it.

It is like when you have a bad fever; a time comes when the fever breaks, and although you still have all the aches and pains and your head still hurts, deep inside an easing begins without your having to do anything to make it happen. One knows one is on the mend.

**When you see something, shine through it.**

In shining through, one sees the dreamlike quality of phenomena, one sees it is a dream; or, alternatively, one sees that we are all always in samadhi. The light is behind the scrim.

Koan number 42 of the *Mumonkan* tells of a woman in samadhi sitting close to Buddha. Regrettably, in those days, most Buddhists believed that women were not capable of following the Buddha's way. (This was not the case among Zen Buddhists, and many Zen stories tell of women besting one or another of the masters.) In this koan, Manjushri protests to Buddha, asking why a woman—who represents the ignorant mind—can sit so close to the Buddha. Buddha tells Manjushri to bring the woman out of samadhi and ask her for himself. Manjushri was unable to do so. Buddha then calls upon Momyo, who lived many thousands of miles away from Buddha, and told him to bring the woman out of samadhi.

We are always in samadhi. Samadhi supports the world. Our samadhi is the mirror in which the world is suspended. Now, as we sit in this room, we are in samadhi. We cannot "get out" of samadhi. This is the point of this koan. Manjushri, the very essence of wisdom—in the koan it says he was the teacher of the seven legendary Buddhas—could not get the woman out of samadhi. It took Momyo, the intellect, to do so. The intellect, with its concepts and logic, hides our true nature and gives us the appearance of living in a world that is apart from us. We seem to be no longer in samadhi. "Shining through" is seeing into the samadhi-quality, going beyond the thingness of things. When we see into the *dharmakaya*, we see that "form is emptiness"; now we see that "emptiness is form."

**If you fall into adverse situations, then shine through adverse situations.**

When you are thrown into turmoil, when everyone starts running around in circles and you are the center of it, then, even at that moment, you must struggle somehow to bring your awakening into focus and shine through that very turmoil. At first it will seem like trying to shine through mud. One tries repeatedly, and all one can get is the bitterness, the pain, and the frustration of the situation. Nevertheless, one must go on and eventually even the leaden quality of life yields to this shining through. This leaden quality, too, is part of the dream; it too has no self-nature.

We play a trick on ourselves by seeing happiness as fleeting, as having no substance, and by seeing our sorrows and sadness as having substance and permanence. In a very subtle way, we begin to invest more and more in our pain and suffering. We come to prize our suffering as an anchor. I remember counseling a woman who, one day, suddenly turned to me and said, "You know, working to give up my neurosis gives my life meaning. I cannot give up my neurosis. If I do my life will have no meaning." This is why we find people for whom suffering is an art form; for them, the last refuge of all is their suffering. To shine through suffering is much more difficult than to shine through happiness, not only because happiness is by its very nature shining, but because it seems to us that we are giving up our last refuge.

This is one of the problems of emphasizing the truth that suffering is the way. It can reinforce people's belief that suffering is in someway fundamentally real in itself and a rock on which to build. Many more people build on misery than build on happiness. The Christian Church may be built upon Peter, the rock, but Peter stands on the suffering of Christ. We are encouraged to enter vicariously into this suffering. Gurdjieff said that the last thing people are prepared to surrender is their suffering. Many people seek, not to get rid of their suffering, but the opportunity to talk about it, to air it, to display it. Some people have art exhibitions; others have suffering exhibitions. It gives their life meaning.

**When greed or desire arise, shine though greed and desire; when hatred or anger arise, shine through hatred and anger; when you act out of ignorance, shine through ignorance.**

People say, "But wait a moment, this man is awakened, this woman is awakened—how come they've got anger and hatred?" It is because work still has to be done. Anger and hatred are the steel reinforcements in the concrete of our ego. These have enabled us to withstand the shocks of death, of terror, of oppression, of tyranny. Now we have to melt them down. This is so, even after a deep awakening. Sometimes anger and rage are so deeply buried that someone does not even know they know they have them—then something comes up, a new situation has to be faced, some karmic debt must be repaid, and they explode.

**At all times, in all places, be it desires, senses, gain, loss, right, wrong, visions of Buddha or of dharma, in all things shine through with your whole body.**

Instead of using the expression "to shine through," one could use the expression "to smile through." After newcomers have attended a beginners' workshop at the Montreal Zen Center, we invite them to attend a beginners' course. They are given further instruction, have several short periods of meditation, and their questions are answered as far as it is possible to answer them. We put emphasis on the importance of practice in everyday life. At the end of each evening of the course, we give the participants a simple exercise to encourage them to remain alert and present during the following week. The exercise is like an alarm clock to awaken them from their dream of duality during the day. One of the exercises is based upon koan number 6 of the *Mumonkan,* "Buddha holds up a flower." Part of the koan reads, "Long ago, when Buddha was at Vulture Peak to give a talk, he held up a flower before the assembly. All remained silent except the venerable Mahakashyapa, who smiled."

I talk to the group about three different kinds of smiles. You will see the first kind at the airport when someone sees a loved one coming through the arrivals door. A great smile breaks out on both of their faces. They then embrace: the smile is already an embrace. The second kind of smile you will see on the face a student. The class has been given a problem to work on. The students sit with furrowed brows trying to solve the problem. Suddenly, one of them gets it. A broad smile breaks out on her face. Both of these two smiles have something in common. The first smile is an embrace, becoming one with another. A child given a present at Christmas will smile this way as she hugs her present. The second is also a becoming one, this time through comprehension. Comprehension means holding together ( *com,* together; *prehension,* to hold). A third kind of smile yet is possible. This is the smile of Mahakashyapa. I ask the group, "What is this smile?"

We have a number of expressions in which shining light and the smile are brought together. For example, we say, "Her face lit up with a smile," "She has a sunny smile," "She has a bright smile," "Her face was shining," or "Her face was beaming," meaning that she was smiling. We have already shown the connection between light and our true nature. In the Old Testament, it says that when Moses came down from the mountain after his encounter with Jehovah, his face was shining.

The smile, if it is genuine, is an opening onto wholeness, holiness, health—these three words have a common etymology. A number of different researchers have shown the connection between laughter and health. Possibly the most famous of these is anecdotal but interesting. Norman Cousins, who was the editor of a national magazine, was diagnosed as having an incurable illness. He collected together films, books, and cartoons and treated himself to a couple of months' laughter. His illness went away; he was made whole.

Moses met Jehovah. I could equally well have said that he encountered the holy, or the whole, One. It was the one that shone through his face in the same way that the one shines through beaming face of a child at Christmas. To shine through, to smile through, is to allow unity to manifest.

Three different kinds of smile are possible. The smile brought about by unity with the outside, the smile brought about by unity inside, and Mahakashyapa's smile. One sees this smile on icons and pictures of bodhisattvas, particularly the bodhisattva Kannon. This smile shines through.

Unfortunately the smile, like so much else in our society, has been abused. Secondhand car salespeople, Pepsodent adverts, indeed, all the dreary commercials that assault one daily on television have pictures of "smiling" people. It is only the people in the commercials who use the competitors' products who ever have a frown. The little yellow button with two dots and a curve proliferated during the sixties and trivialized the smile.

You do not have to be awakened to shine through. You can maintain a half smile on your face. Others will not immediately recognize this smile, but it is not for others that you smile. While waiting in line at the bank or the checkout counter, or while stuck in the traffic, if you can let a half smile appear on your lips, some of the tension and irritation will melt, making it easier to be patient.

You can also make anxiety and depression smile. When we

suffer, we have two pains: the pain that comes from the situation, and the pain that comes from "I hurt!" For example, the company that you work for may be letting several of its employees go. "Downsizing," it is now called. You wonder, "Will I have to go?" This wondering is natural. You can add up the pros and cons and think through the problem. Then you worry, How will I pay the mortgage? What will others think? Will I be able to get another job? and so on. These thoughts swirl around without ever really being formulated into real questions. The first kind of thinking about the problem is painful. The second is also painful. One cannot do anything about the first kind of pain. Being fired is painful. The second kind of pain, which also often includes "Why me?" is the pain "I hurt," and can be reduced.

Most people try to suppress both kinds of pain, or else confuse them and so create a vicious cycle between them. This is like holding a microphone against a loudspeaker. But by allowing the pain to smile, the second kind of pain is reduced, making the whole situation easier to bear. This is shining through.

**If you do not fall back, the karma created by your former actions will dissolve naturally. You will be liberated in a way that cannot be imagined.**

If we continue shining through in this way, then a subtle change occurs in our practice. Shining through is no longer intentional, it is no longer a "practice." A master responded to the koan, "How do you take a step from the top of a hundred-foot pole?" by saying, "On top of the hundred-foot pole an iron cow gives birth to a calf." This is how it is; it is natural. The cold, hard iron naturally gives birth to the warm life of the smile. This is not contradictory. "An iron cow gives birth" is the simplest way to describe naturally smiling through. Essence and appearance interfuse perfectly. What was a cul-de-sac that blocked and stymied, now becomes an open meadow in which you can run and skip. The iron tree blooms and a wall that was once a thousand feet thick is now just a sunlit path. We enter the realm of the indescribable. One sees the whole world is made of knowing/being, the whole world is *bodhi*, the whole world is light.

> *Gate, gate, paragate, parasamgate, bodhi, svaha!*
> Gone, gone, gone beyond, gone quite beyond,
> just *bodhi*, just knowing, rejoice!

**The way you act will conform to how you understand. Host and guest will merge completely. Body and mind will no longer be two, and what you are and the way you appear will not obstruct each other. Getting to the state of true equanimity is called knowing equality as the nature of reality.**

This seems to be very similar to samadhi that can be attained through practice, but that is evanescent. Although the way things are seen in samadhi attained through practice, and the way they are seen through knowing equality are the same in principle, in fact they are very different. What is called "knowing equality as the nature of reality," refers to freedom that has been made possible by constantly refining one's state and so allowing samadhi to shine through. On the one hand, Hakuin says that after the samadhi one has attained through practice, if involved in situations brought about by habit patterns and conflicts, one will not have developed the insight or the strength to be able to cope with them. Therefore one will be caught up in those situations and will not be free. Hakuin calls this refined practice after awakening "knowing equality to be the nature of reality."

**This way of knowing is associated with the southerly direction and called the Gate of Practice. It is like when the sun is in the south, its light is full and brings light to all the hidden places in the deep valleys, melting even the most solid ice and drying the ground however wet. Although a bodhisattva has the eye to see reality (kensho), unless you go through this gate of practice, you cannot clear away obstructions brought about by afflictions and actions and therefore cannot attain to the state of liberation and freedom. What a pity that would be, what a loss.**

Hakuin is saying that once one has been able to work with shining through, the sun's warmth is able to get to dark places. The sun begins unfreezing, unblocking, and smoothing out. Another analogy would be the following: I used to paint in oils, whose base was turpentine. Sometimes I would inadvertently leave a brush without cleaning it. Then, some time later, I would want to do some more painting, only to find the brush as hard as a rock. I would get a jar of clean turpentine and stand the brush in it. Little by little, the turpentine eats its way into the paint on the brush.

I could, of course, have hammered the brush with a hammer, and I would have got a few little tufts of hair at the end, a quarter of an inch or so, that I might have been able to use to apply the paint. But, if I stand it in the turpentine, although will take longer, nevertheless the turpentine dissolves the paint and gradually the hairs separate and become malleable and soft.

It doesn't happen all at once, but it happens. This is because the basis of the paint is turpentine. Mahakashyapa's smile, or the unity of knowing that shines through, provides the "turpentine." If the basis of all is knowing, if the substance of all is one knowing, by allowing knowing to pervade the crust of habitual reactions, mental blocks, and cul-de-sacs, they all will eventually dissolve into knowing.

## The Gate of Awakening

**After you have reached the nondual realm of equality of reality, it is essential that you then clearly understand the awakened ones' profound principle of differentiation. After this you must master the methods for helping sentient beings. Otherwise, even though you have developed and attained unhindered knowing, you will, nevertheless, remain in the nest of the Hinayana and will be unable to realize total, unobstructed knowing. You will lack freedom to change in any required way to help sentient beings, to awaken yourself and others, and reach the ultimate Great Awakening where awareness and action are completely perfect.**

We go up the mountain for ourselves; we come down the mountain for others. Seeing into the *dharmakaya* and the *sambhogakaya,* seeing into the emptiness and oneness of all, is going up the mountain; this we do for ourselves. If we climb the mountain to stay there, if we work simply to step off the wheel of birth and death, we then remain in the nest of the Hinayanists. We must come down the mountain. Now we must understand in such a way that we can make sense of it for others. Furthermore, we must be able to act in a spontaneous, creative way so that our whole life is a service for others. We then cannot help but serve others. This spontaneity, this freedom, is at play for others. At this point in Hakuin's exposition, in view of the long road that he has mapped out, we begin to have sympathy with the notion that we must live many lives to attain true Buddhahood. Nevertheless, we have undertaken to do this work, and it must be done, no matter how inadequately or imperfectly we seem to be doing it.

Let me say something about spontaneity. Some people tend to think that spontaneity is having a minimum reaction time—you say something, and someone responds even before the words have left your mouth. He goes off like a firecracker. However, a short fuse is not what is at issue here. Spontaneity occurs after we have become so totally integrated that self and other are no more. Life is just one continuous flow. This comes after much work, much conscious labor and intentional suffering. If we try to force spontaneity or pretend we have it, we play at Zen, and this will inhibit authentic unfolding.

A monk asked Joshu, "I am new at the monastery, please teach me."

Joshu asked, "Have you had breakfast?"

"Yes," replied the monk.

"Then wash your bowls."

**This is why one must arouse an attitude of deep compassion and commitment to help all sentient beings everywhere.**

This is another strange statement, and people ask, "Doesn't awakening bring with it in its wake compassion?" The answer is yes and no. It does, but like understanding, it too has to be nurtured. In the same way that we have to really commit ourselves to shining through, we must commit ourselves to compassion. To shine through means we must be ready to stand in the midst of the furnace while it burns and blazes around us without trying to run away, without trying to move. As we burn, we see through the burning, and it is very painful. Great commitment is necessary. In the same way, we have to make an intense commitment to compassion, to be willing to be one with others. Unless we can do this, we stay at the top of the mountain and are never entirely free. We are always slightly superior, always protecting our awakening. We must reaffirm this commitment to compassion repeatedly. This is why chanting the bodhisattva's four vows is so important.

> All beings without number, I vow to liberate,
> Endless blind passions, I vow to uproot,
> Dharma gates beyond measure, I vow to penetrate,
> The Great Way of Buddha, I vow to attain.

Hakuin has given us what appears to be an agenda for lifetimes, and the task is huge. Yet, when you look at the magnificence of the freedom and compassion that is available to each of us, when you realize that as human beings we are seeds in potential that can grow into huge trees in which all kinds of beings can find shelter, then you expect the price to be high. The work Hakuin has set out is of cosmic proportions. Once we have entered the Way, we have already transcended what it means to be simply human. In the second koan of the *Mumonkan*, the koan on the importance of karma, the monk says, "I am not a human being." Although totally grounded in the human, our practice nevertheless transcends this human condition. It doesn't matter whether we walk this way alone, with another, with a few others, or with hundreds of others. Once one enters the Buddha's Way, everything is taken care of; once we enter the way of truth, of true compassion, no matter how far we may be from its realization and manifestation, everything is taken care of. We need no longer question how much time or how little time; our work is not of this order. When we are looking, searching into the question "Who am I?"; when we are struggling to stay with our breath, following the breath, being one with the breath; when we are struggling to see into koans; this is like the growth of a tree. The tree is growing, spreading, developing. The roots dig deep into the teaching. The sap of the tree is faith, and faith is available in abundance. What is needed to nurture the growth of this great tree is not lacking.

**To begin with, you should study day and night the verbal teachings of the Buddha and patriarchs so that you can penetrate the principles of things in their infinite variety. Ascertain and analyze, one by one, the profundities of the five houses and the seven schools of Zen and the wondrous doctrines of the eight teachings given in the five periods of Buddha's teaching career.**

Originally, five houses of Zen came into existence. In *Zen Dust* these are said to be the Hinayana, Quasi-Mahayana, Complete Mahayana, the Sudden Teaching, and the One Vehicle, or Hua-yen. Others, for example Charles Luk, give the five houses as Igyo Zen, Rinzai Zen, Soto Zen, Ummon Zen, and Hogen Zen. But these classifications need not bother us too much. Only two of these remain as viable schools, the Soto and the Rinzai. In Japan the distinction between these two schools is taken very seriously. Yasutani Roshi, the first master with whom I studied, was considered to be a traitor for having left the Soto sect. Indeed, one Japanese teacher that I met said he was mad!

The main distinction between the two schools is that the Soto tradition says that we need not strive to come to awakening. We are already whole and complete, and all striving will simply lead us further from the truth. The main practice of Soto is *shikantaza,* which means "just sitting." Sitting in zazen is already awakening. Some Soto teachers tend to reject the Rinzai teaching, which encourages active pursuit of enlightenment, saying that this way is a way of grabbing at awakening, and comes from spiritual ambition.

Rinzai Gigen, the founder of the Rinzai school, would be in full agreement with the Soto teachers in saying that nothing needs to be done. He said, for example, "Followers of the Way, right now the resolute man knows full well that from the beginning, there is nothing to do. Only because your faith [in this] is insufficient do you ceaselessly chase about; having thrown away your head, you go on looking for it, unable to stop yourself."[36] He also said later, "Followers of the Way, true sincerity is extremely difficult to attain, and the Buddhadharma is deep and mysterious."[37]

One of the things that Rinzai Zen insists upon is the importance of kensho, seeing into one's true nature. Kensho is the source of the four ways of knowing; they are ultimately derived from kensho. Many Soto teachers reject this and say that kensho is not only unnecessary but is itself illusory. Nevertheless, as I said in the introduction, Zen master Keizan, who is considered to be the great patriarch of the Soto Zen Sect, said, "Even if well-versed in theory and enlightened in the Way, you are wandering until you have gained *satori,* which is like the Emperor's seal on goods, proof that they are neither contraband nor poisonous." He goes on to say, "Though there is nothing to give or receive, *satori* should be as conclusive as knowing your face by touching the nose." Finally, he says, "Always remember that your Original Mind, calm and lucid, awaits discovery."[38]

So we should not see Soto and Rinzai as in any way in conflict. Provided the teacher has come to awakening, it does not matter the kind of emphasis he or she places on different aspects of the teaching. Any teacher who is teaching authentically is teaching from his or her own experience, not from some theory or study of Buddhist texts. If, after awakening, one reads the teachings of Hakuin, Dogen, Ta-hui, or Keizan, one does so for their inspiration, and for the confirmation that they give of one's own light, not to find the truth.

A principle worth remembering is that if one is going to practice Rinzai Zen authentically, then one must be a good Soto practitioner; and if one is going to practice Soto Zen authentically, then one must be a good Rinzai practitioner. Bearing this principle in mind, one will not go far wrong.

If you have any energy left over, you should clarify
the deep principles of the various different philosophies.
However, if this and that get to be too much trouble,
it will just waste your energy to no avail. If you
thoroughly investigate the sayings of the Buddhas
and patriarchs that are difficult to pass through,
and clearly arrive at their essential meaning, perfect
understanding will shine forth and the principles of
all things should naturally be completely clear.
This is called the eye to read the sutras.

Many people think that Zen is "anti-intellectual." From all that Hakuin is now saying, this evidently is not so. If one is familiar with the writings of Dogen, one will realize how much importance Dogen puts on study and thought. The great Korean master Chinul also placed great emphasis on the teachings. The chief problem with intellectual understanding is that one can feel that is sufficient. So often, if one has a good understanding, which is a well-integrated appreciation of what the masters are saying, because one has the sayings of the masters at one's fingertips, one feels one has arrived. The intellectual is like a man in a prison with expandable walls. It seems as though it is no prison at all.

Another problem is that the intellect freezes experience; all that one knows is a series of static images, not the living movement of life. Freezing experience makes it static and absolute in an illusory way. This is why the intellectual is so often arrogant. The illusion of the absolute gives the illusion of a finality. This is why one should read very sparingly until one has seen into one's true nature.

Hakuin himself does not press the point of reading and studying very much because he says, "However, if this and that get to be too much trouble, it will just waste your energy to no avail." He does emphasize koan practice. "The sayings of the Buddhas and patriarchs that are difficult to pass through" are the koans. At the Rochester Zen Center, I passed through a number of preliminary koans and then through the *Mumon-kan* and the *Hekigan-roku* twice. Since then I have worked through and studied all the koans many times over, both on my own and while helping others to work with them. One teacher suggested that koans are like hurdles that the practitioner must leap over and so gain in strength. I tend to look upon koan practice as koan appreciation. You can steadily

deepen your appreciation of the meaning of the koans. It is not
unlike listening to classical music. You might enjoy hearing a
piece of music the first time. When you listen to it again later,
you may well realize that you missed much of the subtlety of
the music the first time around. A third listening shows how
much the music contains. After the tenth hearing, you realize
that this is a very subtle piece of music indeed.

Eventually, one is able to read the sutras as koans, and then
one can truly appreciate the subtlety of the Buddhadharma.

**Now, the verbal teachings of the Buddhas and the
patriarchs are extremely deep, and one should not consider that one has mastered them completely after one
has gone through them once or twice. When you climb
a mountain, the higher you climb, the higher they are;
when you go into the ocean, the farther you go, the
deeper it is. It is the same in this case. It is also like forging iron to make a sword; it is considered best to put it
into the forge over and over, refining it again and again.
Though it is always the same forge, unless you put the
sword in over and over and refine it a hundred times,
it can hardly turn out to be a fine sword.**

The forge, or furnace, is a favorite metaphor for the labor of
the spirit. The alchemists use this metaphor also. The first step
in alchemy is to make a hermetically sealed vessel. It must be
sealed tight, otherwise it will leak when subjected to the intense
heat of the furnace. The Catholic religion also talks of the fires
of purgatory. It is in these fires that the soul is purified.

**Penetrating study is also like this; unless you enter the
great forge of the Buddha and patriarchs, difficult to**

pass through, and make repeated efforts at refinement, through suffering and pain, total and independent knowing cannot come forth. Penetrating through the barriers of the Buddha and patriarchs over and over again, responding to beings' potential everywhere with mastery and freedom of technique, is called subtle, observing, discerning knowing.

Why is spiritual work painful? Why does Gurdjieff say that his way is the way of conscious labor and intentional suffering? Why is the central figure of Christianity the icon of a man on a cross? St. Julian of Norwich prayed for some serious illness by which she could work for God. People have undertaken miles of pilgrimage carrying different kinds of burdens, crawling on their knees, or even rolling. Hsu Yun, a great contemporary spiritual teacher, made a pilgrimage of a thousand miles taking one step and performing three full prostrations. During the retreats that we conduct here, most of the participants suffer, at one time or another during the *sesshin*, intense pain. What is the point of this?

As we have said, with suffering there are two sufferings. In the forge of the masters, "I hurt" is purged away, and the dualism that strangles our life begins to lose its grip.

**You do not investigate by means of intellectual considerations.**

The limitations of the intellect are most obvious when one works on the koans. A monk asked Tozan, "What is Buddha?" Tozan replied, "Three pounds of flax!" What can the intellect do with that? The Zen mind is a creative mind, or, better still, it is creativity. Creativity is shocking, dynamic, without precedent. Intellectual activity is linear; the conclusion follows from the premises. It is essentially static. This is because it deals with concepts, static images. Because the conclusion follows from the premises, logical reasoning corresponds to what was expected. Koans awaken the mind to its intrinsic, creative nature. When one reads the responses the Zen masters gave their students, one must admire not only how creative, but also how apt and alive, these responses were. The intellect can only give dead words.

**This way of knowing, to save yourself and to liberate others, when completely fulfilled and mastered, is subtle, observing, discerning knowing.**

I have used the word *differentiation* for this way of knowing. The expression "subtle, observing, discerning knowing" is also very good, although somewhat clumsy. Perhaps just *discernment* would be best. To appreciate the subtlety of an argument means that one has a finely developed discernment. An artist who appreciates the subtlety of color likewise has a keen discernment. Yasutani Roshi said, "Even a cracked cup is perfect." One of the more famous and misunderstood of all Zen sayings is, "Tall bamboo is tall; short bamboo is short." This too is subtle, observing, discerning knowing. The koan that goes most directly to the heart of the matter is koan number 26 of the *Mumonkan,* which I mentioned earlier: "When the monks assembled before the midday meal to listen to his lecture, Hogen pointed at the bamboo blinds. Two monks simultaneously went and rolled them up. Hogen said, 'One has it, the other doesn't.'"

This is the state of the perfectly fulfilled body of reward; it is associated with the westerly direction and called the Gate of Awakening. It is like the sun having passed the high noon, gradually sinking toward the west. While the great way of knowing of equality is right in the middle, the faculties of sentient beings cannot be seen and the teachings of differentiation among things cannot be made clear. If you do not stop in the realm of self-enlightenment as inner realization but, instead, cultivate this subtle, observing, discerning knowing, you have done what you can do; having done your task, you can reach the land of rest.

What is "the land of rest"? A koan from the *Hekigan-roku* tells of it: A monk asked Zen master Kyorin, "What is the meaning of Bodhidharma's coming from the West?" Kyorin answered, "Sitting long, getting tired."

This haiku by Basho also points to its meaning:

The shell of a cicada.
It sang itself
utterly away.

This rest is not what the setting sun means; it means that you have accomplished all the ways of knowing, have fulfilled awakening, because awakening self and others, fulfillment of awareness and action, is considered real ultimate awakening.

## The Gate of Nirvana

This is the secret gateway to the command of the mind and is the realm of ultimate liberation. This is knowing without any kind of defilement, a virtue that is not created. If you do not realize this way of knowing, you will not be able to do freely what must be done to benefit yourself and others. It is the effortless way.

Master Sekito said to the layman, "Since we last met, what have you been doing during the day?"

"When you ask me about what I have been doing, I can't open my mouth," the layman replied.

"That is why I am asking you," said Sekito. Whereupon the layman offered this verse:

> I do nothing unusual during the day,
> I just happen to be in harmony with things.
> Grasping nothing, getting rid of nothing,
> There's no obstruction, no conflict anywhere.
> What is exalted in that?
> From off the hills and mountains,
> The last speck of dust is cleared away.
> My miraculous power and magical activity:
> Drawing water and carrying wood for the fire.

Because the preceding way of knowing by differentiation is gained through correct practice, it is in the realm of cultivation: realization is gained by practice. It is therefore a way of knowing that is reached through effort. The way of knowing perfect action transcends the bounds of practice, realization, and attainment through study. It is beyond any kind of demonstration or explanation.

A master said, "I do nothing all day, but nothing is left undone." A famous *sumi-e* painting (a traditional Japanese ink brush painting) puts what Hakuin has just said in a nutshell: it shows a Zen master fast asleep, leaning on a tiger.

One could say that knowing by way of differentiation is like the flower of complete awakening; practice is this flower coming into bloom. On the other hand, with knowing and "doing what needs to be done," the flower of full awakening and practice drops away and the fruit ripens. You cannot possibly see this even in a dream unless you have passed through the final stages of transcendence of our school. That is why it is said that at the last word, you finally come to the impenetrable barrier.

The way to point out the direction is not in verbal explanations; if you want to reach this realm, just refine your subtle, discerning knowing through the differentiating and difficult-to-pass-through koans, smelting and forging hundreds of times, over and over. Even if you have passed through some, repeat them over and over, examining meticulously—what is this little truth beyond all convention in the great matter of transcendence? If you do not regress in your examination of the sayings of the ancients, someday you may come to know this bit of wonder.

A monk asked Joshu, "Does a dog have the Buddha-nature?" Joshu replied "*Mu!*"

**Even so, if you do not seek an awakened master and personally enter his forge, you cannot plumb the profound subtleties.**

The way is full of pitfalls, cul-de-sacs, barriers, and abysses. Fool's gold is strewn along the way. On the path many different kinds of experiences, awakenings, and samadhis can be encountered. Some are memorable, some transforming. It is not that one needs a teacher to confirm one's awakening, but to cut away illusory awakenings and strip away the burden of fool's gold.

Awakening has a number of signs that all can recognize, but a master can see in an instant beyond all these signs into the heart. Awakening is always sudden. Awakening is awakening to the wholeness, the One bright pearl; one cannot awaken in halves or quarters. Awakening has no content; one awakens to unreflected knowing. This is why Dogen tells us that an awakened person does not know he or she is awakened. God does not know he is God. Awakening brings peace beyond understanding, ultimate satisfaction. Awakening is intimate; one speaks of it with great reluctance. Awakening brings with it a renewed and deep desire for practice.

**The only worry is that real teachers of Zen are extremely few and hard to find.**

If that were true in Hakuin's time, it is even more so in ours. False teachers are abundant. Some have had awakening; most have not. Those who have had awakening, if they have not entered the forge of the master, have not been able to make the awakening work for them and so it remains but a memory, regurgitated endlessly and mercilessly. Among those so-called teachers who have not come to awakening are many that would deny the value, even the fact, of awakening itself. Such teachers build obstacles in the mind of their followers, which prevent them from allowing the light of the true self to shine through.

The more popular a teacher is, the less likely he or she will be authentic. True spiritual work requires, as Gurdjieff reminded us, conscious labor and intentional suffering. As noted earlier, Dogen said much the same thing: "Everything is exertion. To attempt to avoid exertion is an impossible evasion because the attempt itself is exertion." But, as he also said, "This sustained exertion is not something which people of the world naturally love or desire, yet it is the last refuge of all."

The inauthentic teacher will trade in sentimentality in the place of genuine feeling. Sentimentality, as Oscar Wilde pointed out, is indulging in an emotion for which one has not paid the price. This kind of teacher will use what Harada Roshi called "powder and rouge" expressions and will liberally sprinkle his or her writings with words such as *love, peace, compassion,* and *joy,* like chocolate chips on an ice cream. They will walk slowly and majestically and have a voice that purrs like a cat. Hakuin wrote a verse "that pours scorn on this odious race of pseudo-priests"[39]:

> Earth's vilest thing? From which all men recoil?
> Crumbly charcoal? Firewood that's wet? Watered
>   lamp oil?
> A cartman? A boatman? A stepmother? Skunks?
> Mosquitoes? Lice? Blueflies? Rats? Thieving monks.

But if someone exerts his energy to the utmost in this, and penetrates through clearly, he attains freedom in all ways, transcends the realms of Buddhas and devils, resolves sticking points, removes bonds, pulls out nails and pegs, and leads people to the realm of purity and ease. This is called the knowing required to accomplish works. It is associated with the northerly direction and is called the Gate of Nirvana. It is like when the sun reaches the northern quarter, when it is midnight and the whole world is dark; reaching the sphere of this knowing is not within understanding or comprehension—even Buddhas can't see, much less outsiders and devils.

Who walks? Who talks? People often reply, "I do. I walk. I talk." Yes, of course, but who is this "I"? So much is taken for granted. We strain at gnats, but swallow elephants whole. "Which muscle are you going to use first to walk?" Is it not marvelous? One meets a friend and tells her all that has been happening. The right words flow out, in the right order, with the right emphasis. Sometimes the speaker is bilingual, even trilingual. Yet, the languages are not mixed up. How does one do that? Who speaks? Of course, the behaviorists say the question is unnecessary: no one speaks. Yet the Zen Buddhist would say the same.

> No one walks along this path
> This autumn evening.

Who, though, is this *no one*? The alchemists say, "Our sun is a dark sun." Not even Buddha can see who walks, who talks. But, "Who walks? Who talks?"

**This is the thoroughly peaceful state of pure reality of the Buddhas and patriarchs.**

To quote Nisargadatta Maharaj once again, "My body is peace and silence."

Koan 40 of the *Hekigan-roku* points to the peace of pure reality:

> Hearing, seeing, touching, and knowing are not one
> and one;
> Mountains and rivers are not to be seen in a mirror.
> The frosty sky, the setting moon at midnight;
> With whom will the serene waters of the lake reflect the
> shadows in the cold?[40]

**This is called great nirvana, replete with four attributes (self, purity, bliss, and eternity). It is also called knowing the essential nature of the cosmos, in which the four ways of knowing are fully complete. The center means harmonizing the four ways of knowing into a whole, and the essential nature of the cosmos means the king of awakening, master of the teachings, being king of the dharma, free in all ways.**

**I hope that you Buddhists of great faith will arouse great trust and commitment and develop the great practice for the realization of these four ways of knowing and true awakening. Do not forgo the great matter of countless ages just because of pride in your present view.**

# Notes

....

## Introduction

1. Norman Waddell, trans., *Wild Ivy: The Spiritual Autobiography of Zen Master Hakuin* (Boston: Shambhala Publications, 1999), 1.
2. Norman Waddell, trans., *The Essential Teachings of Zen Master Hakuin* (Boston: Shambhala Publications, 1994), 27.
3. Lucien Stryk and Takashi Ikemoto, ed. and trans., *Zen: Poems, Prayers, Sermons, Anecdotes, Interviews* (New York: Doubleday, 1965), 49.
4. Waddell, *Essential Teachings of Zen Master Hakuin*, 45.
5. Ibid., 13.
6. Mathew 23: 13,15.
7. Waddell, *Essential Teachings of Zen Master Hakuin*, 72.
8. Ibid., 24.
9. The full "*Mu*" koan reads: "A monk asked Zen master Joshu, 'Does a dog have the Buddha-nature?' Joshu replied '*Mu!*' ('No!')" For more on this and the other breakthrough koans, see Albert Low, *The World a Gateway: Commentaries on the Mumonkan* (Boston: Charles Tuttle, 1995), 25.
10. Waddell, *Wild Ivy*, xxx.
11. Ibid., xxxi.
12. Ibid., 10.
13. Ibid., 18.
14. Ibid.
15. Philip Yampolsky, trans., *The Zen Master Hakuin: Selected Writings* (New York: Columbia Univ. Press, 1971), 118.
16. Ibid.
17. Ibid.
18. Ibid.
19. Ibid., 118–19.
20. Ibid., 119.
21. Ibid.
22. Ibid., 120.
23. Ibid.
24. For more on this, see Albert Low, *An Invitation to Practice Zen* (Rutland, Vt.: Tuttle Publishing, 1989).

25. Albert Low, *Creating Consciousness: A Study in Creativity, Consciousness, Evolution, and Violence* (Ashland, Ore. White Cloud Press, 2001).

26. Sharon Begley, "God and the Brain: How We Are Wired for Spirituality," *Newsweek*, May 7, 2001, p. 53.

27. For more on the dualism within samadhi, see Albert Low, *The Butterfly's Dream* (Rutland, Vt.: Tuttle Publishing, 1993), 134–42.

28. Translation by Albert Low.

29. Waddell, *Wild Ivy*, 65.

## INTRODUCTION TO THE TEXT

1. Thomas Cleary, trans. and ed., *The Original Face: An Anthology of Rinzai Zen* (New York: Grove Press, 1978), 130–40.

2. Isshu Miura and Ruth Fuller Sasaki, *Zen Dust: The History of the Koan and Koan-Study in Rinzai (Lin-chi) Zen* (New York: Harcourt, Brace, and World, 1966), 311.

3. Low, *The World a Gateway*, 183.

4. For more on this, see Albert Low, *Zen and the Sutras* (North Clarendon, Vt.: Tuttle Publishing, 2000).

5. For more on this, see Miura and Fuller Sasaki, *Zen Dust*, 314.

6. The eight consciousnesses are the *alaya, vijnana,* the *manas, manovijnana,* and the five senses. For more on this see Albert Low, *Zen and the Sutras*, 13–34.

7. Miura and Fuller Sasaki, *Zen Dust*, 314.

8. Ruth Fuller Sasaki, trans., *The Recoded Sayings of Ch'an Master Lin-chi Hui-chao of Chen Prefecture* (Kyoto: The Institute for Zen Studies, 1975), 8.

9. Yampolsky, *Zen Master Hakuin: Selected Writings*, 49.

10. Ibid., 35.

11. Ibid.

12. Ibid.

13. Ibid.

14. Ibid., 36.

15. Ibid., 37.

16. Ibid.

17. Ibid., 38.

18. Cleary, *Original Face*.

## *The Four Ways of Knowing of an Awakened Person*: HAKUIN'S TEXT

1. The three bodies are: the *dharmakaya,* the *sambhokakaya,* and the *nirmanakaya.*

2. *Sarva,* whole, complete, everything; *jna,* primordial knowing.
3. This means all the Buddhist teachings.

## COMMENTARY ON
### *The Four Ways of Knowing of an Awakened Person*

1. Miura and Fuller Sasaki, *Zen Dust,* 66.
2. A distinction must be made between samadhi that can be attained through one pointed concentration and samadhi that is our natural state, known also as "the ground of pure enlightenment of sentient beings. . . ." *The Sutra of Perfect Enlightenment: Korean Buddhism's Guide to Meditation.*
3. Traditionally, the breakthrough koans are the following: "*Mu!*" "What is your face before your parents were born?" and "What is the sound of one hand clapping?"
4. Low, *Zen and the Sutras,* 62.
5. Waddell, *Essential Teachings of Zen Master Hakuin,* 30.
6. Ibid.
7. Ibid.
8. Sarvepalli Radhakrishnan, ed. and trans., *The Bhagavad Gita* (London: George Allen and Unwin, 1948), 307.
9. Miura and Fuller Sasaki, *Zen Dust,* 9.
10. Ibid., 66.
11. See Low, *Zen and the Sutras,* 35–56.
12. Chen-chi Chang, *The Practice of Zen* (London: Rider and Company, 1959), 106.
13. For more on the eighth level of consciousness see Low, *Zen and the Sutras,* 116–29.
14. See discussion of koan number 19 of the *Mumonkan* in Low, *The World a Gateway,* 136.
    Joshu asked Nansen, "What is the Way?"
    Nansen answered, "Everyday mind is the Way." [Your ordinary mind is the Way.]
    "How does one get on to it?"
    "The more you pursue it, the more it runs away."
    "How does one know that one is on the Way?"
    "The Way does not belong to knowing or not knowing. Knowing is illusion. Not knowing is lack of discrimination. It is like vast space. Where is there room for this and that, good and bad?"
15. Philip Kapleau, *The Three Pillars of Zen* (New York: Weatherhill, 1966), 181.
16. In Buddhism, blindness is of several kinds. There are those who can't see, those who won't see, those blinded by light, and there are those

who do not see anything because nothing stands out; all is equal. This is the blindness of Buddha.

17. It is as Hakuin said in his *Chant in Praise of Zazen*, "What is there outside us, what is there we lack?"
18. Kapleau, *Three Pillars of Zen*, 74.
19. Stryk and Ikemoto, *Zen*, 13.
20. The awakened state.
21. Alive words.
22. John C. H. Wu, *The Golden Age of Zen* (Taipei: National War College, 1967), 162.
23. See Paul Demiéville, "The Mirror of the Mind," in Peter N. Gregory, ed., *Sudden and Gradual: Approaches to Enlightenment in Chinese Thought* (Honolulu: Univ. of Hawaii Press, 1987), 13–40.
24. Ibid., 22.
25. Masumi Shibata, trans. and ed., *Passe Sans Porte* (Paris: Villain et Belhomme, 1973), 46. (My translation from the French.)
26. Ibid., 46–47.
27. David Godman, ed., *Be As You Are: The Teachings of Sri Ramana Maharshi* (London: Arkana, 1985), 59.
28. Maurice Frydman, trans., and Sudhakar S. Dikshit, ed., *I am That: Talks with Sri Mahraj Nisargadatta Maharaj* (Durham, N.C.: Acorn Press, 1973), 70.
29. Adapted from Hubert Benoit, *The Supreme Doctrine* (London: Routledge and Kegan Paul, 1955), 236.
30. For more on the origin of guilt, see Low, *Butterfly's Dream*, 13–15.
31. Kapleau, *Three Pillars of Zen*, 175.
32. Stryk and Ikemoto, *Zen*, 4.
33. The circle in the ox herding pictures.
34. Robert E. Buswell, Jr., trans., *The Collected Works of Chinul* (Honolulu: Univ. of Hawaii Press, 1983), 144–45.
35. Albert Low, *To Know Yourself* (Boston: Charles Tuttle, 1997), 105.
36. Fuller Sasaki, *Recoded Sayings of Ch'an Master Lin-chi*, 13.
37. Ibid., 28.
38. Stryk and Ikemoto, *Zen*, 49–50.
39. Waddell, *Essential Teachings of Zen Master Hakuin*, 3.
40. Koan number 40 of the *Hekigan-roku*. See Katsuki Sekida, trans. and comm., *Two Zen Classics: Mumonkan and Hekiganroku* (New York: John Weatherhill, 1977), 255.

# Index

Printed in the United States
by Baker & Taylor Publisher Services